Not Without Hope

by
Louise Johnson

Earl Johnson

MAPLE LANE PUBLISHING

MATSQUI, B.C.

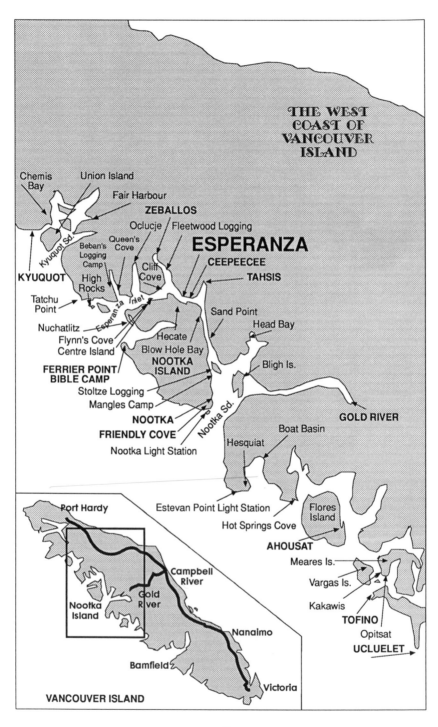

THE WEST
COAST OF
VANCOUVER
ISLAND

Chemis Bay
Union Island
Fair Harbour
ZEBALLOS
Oclucje / Fleetwood Logging
Queen's Cove
Beban's Logging Camp
ESPERANZA
Kyuquot Sd.
CEEPEECEE
KYUQUOT
Cliff Cove
High Rocks
TAHSIS
Tatchu Point
Esperanza Inlet
Sand Point
Nuchatlitz
Head Bay
Flynn's Cove
Centre Island
Hecate
Blow Hole Bay
Bligh Is.
FERRIER POINT / BIBLE CAMP
NOOTKA ISLAND
Stoltze Logging
Mangles Camp
GOLD RIVER
NOOTKA
Nootka Sd.
Boat Basin
FRIENDLY COVE
Nootka Light Station
Hesquiat
Estevan Point Light Station
Flores Island
Hot Springs Cove
AHOUSAT
Meares Is.
Port Hardy
Vargas Is.
Campbell River
Kakawis
Gold River
Nootka Island
TOFINO
Opitsat
Nanaimo
UCLUELET
Bamfield
Victoria
VANCOUVER ISLAND

ii

NOT WITHOUT HOPE

By Louise Johnson

*H*ere is a story about the "early days" on the west coast of Vancouver Island. One man's dream was to serve the people of the coast physically as well as spiritually. Dr. Herman A. McLean established a hospital outpost and mission on a tiny shelf of land in Nootka Sound. He took his wife and family there in 1937 and carved a niche out of the Canadian wilderness which became a haven to the sick and suffering of the region—the loggers, the Indians, the miners, the fishermen. Dr. McLean is one of Canada's great pioneers, and his story had to be told. But, this story is more; it is the story of Mrs. McLean and her family, the staff, the years of service to the community following Dr. McLean's retirement, and it is about the people of the region —their joys, their sorrows.

Here, is a heart-warming story of the first fifty years of the Esperanza community. Louise is a keen observer of people and she has told the story with wit, but also with discretion.

First Printing 1992

ISBN # 0-921966-02-4

Pre-press production by Mediaworks Inc.
Cover design by Chris Kielesinski

MAPLE LANE PUBLISHING

34968 Sim Road
Matsqui, B.C. V0X 1S0

Printed in Canada

Financially assisted by the Province of British Columbia through
the British Columbia Heritage Trust and the B.C. Lottery funds.

DEDICATED TO

Dr. and Mrs. McLean
and their family who gave
hope to the people of the
west coast of Vancouver Island

Acknowledgements

*I*t would be impossible to write a book of this nature without the help of a great number of people. To all of you who were involved I would like to express my gratitude.

I am especially grateful to the McLean family for making this book possible; to my daughter, Nancy Symington, who keyed into her computer the original manuscript from my handwritten and typed notes; to Debra Fieguth who undertook the preliminary editing and who counseled me extensively in writing skills; to Jean Hood who re-typed my original submissions; and to my brother Ed McPherson who came from Ontario to help me complete the manuscript.

I am grateful to those who encouraged me in the early stages, and who prodded me in the latter. Thanks to Phil Hood, my publisher, who believed that this story ought to be written; to my husband, Earl, my mother, Hilda McPherson, and the other members of our families whose continual encouragement gave me both confidence and assurance that the task could be accomplished.

I would like to thank those former staff members who responded to my request for tapes of their experiences, their impressions, and their lessons learned at Esperanza; those who generously submitted stories, letters, clippings, photographs, and other materials; those who agreed to taped interviews of their experiences; and to all those who proof-read the final manuscript for accuracy and authenticity.

As you can imagine, I have gathered a considerable volume of research material. It is unfortunate that more of this could not have been used; however, due to the constraints of book-size, much material had to be synthesized or omitted altogether.

So, to many of you who have spent much time and trouble in preparing and assembling material to send to me, and who do not find it in the story, please forgive me. To those people who feel that certain events or people have been overlooked or omitted or excluded, I beg your forgiveness.

Finally, I thank all the people of the coast whom I have had the pleasure of knowing, who have opened their hearts to me, and who have taught me so much about life "in a tough place".

Above all, I thank God for helping me to tell the story.

Louise Johnson, April 1990

About Louise Johnson

Louise Johnson started research on this book over ten years ago; however, due to her illness and other activities, work on this book was unexpectedly prolonged. One of her dreams fullfilled was the co-ordination and writing of the "Esperanza Cookbook", which was published in 1989. Louise passed away in June of 1990, and this book is published post-humously. Louise would be pleased.

Contents

Historical

Background

*T*he community of Esperanza is situated in Nootka Sound on the west coast of Vancouver Island, approximately 75 miles northwest of Tofino, or about 150 miles up the coast from Victoria. It is accessible only by boat or floatplane.

Nootka Sound is the central sound of the five bodies of water carved into the outer coast of Vancouver Island. Nootka Island, 25 miles long, lies in the midst of Nootka Sound. Surrounding it are deeply indented, finger-like inlets forming fiords hundreds of feet deep. The shoreline is bounded by rock with few landing places for boats, the tides are considerable, the weather unpredictable—a land of inhospitable nature but a land of incredible grandeur.

~~~~~~~~

Over many centuries the only boats that cut through the cool, blue waters of Nootka Sound were the uniquely carved canoes of the West Coast Indian tribes (now called Nuu-chah-nulth). Local to Nootka Sound were the Ehattesahts, Mowachahts, Muchalahts and Nuchatlahts. Their large cedar canoes moved swiftly and easily through both calm and turbulent waters. Each village carved its own distinctive design on the bow. Some had an eagle head while others had a whale, a raven or a wolf. These proud figures identified both villages and families.

The bravery and expertise of the Nuu-chah-nulth men was most evident by the skillful use of their canoes in whale hunting. Months of vigorous preparation were required to equip both body and spirit for the dangerous hunt during whale migrations.

Esperanza (the Spanish word for "hope") is situated in this sound where British Columbia's modern history began. British explorer, Captain James Cook, first named the sound "King George's Sound". He later incorrectly named it "Nootka Sound" thinking that "Nootka" was the Indian name for the area. He raised the British flag on Nootka Island in March, 1778, claiming a European discovery for Great Britain.

Eleven years after Cook set foot on Nootka Island, the Spaniards, led by Don Esteban Jose Martinez, visited and claimed Nootka Island and the surrounding area for the King of Spain. In the struggle that ensued, three British ships were seized by the Spaniards. The Spaniards laid claim to the area from May, 1789 until March, 1795. Juan Francisco de la Bodega y Quadra held the position as governor of Nootka in 1792–93.

During the time of Captain Cook and Don Quadra, Friendly Cove, the main village on Nootka Island, bustled with the activity of an estimated one thousand Indian people. Today, sheltered behind the lighthouse on a large rock are two monuments, one to remember Captain Cook, and the other to remember the day the Spaniards peacefully turned over their claimed rights to the British.

≈≋⊚≋≈

It was into these waters that missionary Percy Wills ventured in the early 1930's aboard the vessel *Otter Point*. Percy was a veteran of the First World War and when he returned to his home in Victoria, B.C., he bore the scars of war not only on his body but also in his heart and mind. The tough army life and all that went along with it left him purposeless, lonely and disillusioned.

Shortly after his return to Canada he listened intently one night to a man preaching the Gospel of Jesus Christ. As he listened, he found himself believing every word the minister was saying. Needing a satisfying purpose in life, Percy felt certain that he was hearing that purpose being spelled out to him.

He had never been a man of half measures and when he decided to live his entire life for Jesus Christ, he meant just that! For ten years he preached in northern Canadian communities, receiving little pay and living in inadequate accommodation. His message however, was powerful in its simplicity, telling about the changes that come when a life is lived in obedience to the God of the Bible. During those years he married Margaret and they became parents of a son and a daughter, Frank and Jean.

Percy was the only Shantyman missionary appointed to Vancouver Island. He was young. He was strong. He had a zeal for the purpose to which he was called. He had travelled with a backpack to the isolated settlements in the rain forests. He had travelled with Indian guides in a canoe into Barkley and Clayoquot Sounds. Now, aboard the *Otter Point,* he and his crew began a two month survey of Nootka Sound to determine the needs of the people in this area. There was a doctor aboard who had recently returned from a mission base in China. He came to help assess the medical needs. Their hearts were broken as they began to realize that the needs of the people were great. Urgent medical care was required. It became evident that many lives could be spared, and much pain controlled if a medical facility and a doctor were made available for this part of the west coast of Vancouver Island.

Percy knelt before the Lord in prayer and earnestly opened his heart, pouring out the need he saw, weeping over the sadness, the pain and the loneliness of the West Coast people. It seemed such a contradiction to Percy. The area was breathtakingly beautiful yet the people were overwhelmed with sickness, despair, severely limited public transportation and no medical help. Without question, in order to effectively share the Gospel here, the Shantymen would have to tend to the people's physical needs first.

As Percy continued to pray for a doctor to come to the West Coast, he returned to his work amongst the logging camps in Port Renfrew, Cowichan Bay, Port Alberni and Great Central Lake. It was the spring of 1937 when word reached Percy about a doctor attending Prairie Bible Institute, Three Hills, Alberta, who had hoped to become a missionary on the west coast. When Percy learned of this incredible possibility, he lost no time in persuading the young man that he had made the right choice, and that Percy had just the right place for him.

That young man was Herman Alexander McLean, M.D. He was God's answer to many prayers.

"Messenger II" at Tahsis Wharf

CHAPTER 1

"This is the place God wants me to be..."

T he woman had heard that a doctor was aboard a boat moored near B.C. Packers at Hecate. It would take nearly six hours over uncertain seas to travel there by boat. Should she risk the trip? Could the doctor do anything for her when she arrived? Her elbow was severely injured and swelling was increasing. A neighbour volunteered, "I'll risk the trip with you; you must see a doctor."

When they arrived, Dr. McLean was ready. To examine the extent of the injury, he found it necessary to administer a local anaesthetic. When the freezing had numbed the area sufficiently for examination, he gently took the woman's painful arm into his skillful hands. His fingers explored the damaged elbow bones.

A helpless feeling came over him as he felt bits of displaced and shattered bone twisting under his fingers. There was no X-ray and no one to consult. After manipulating the elbow and determining the best position for proper healing, he applied a cast. As he worked, he silently called on God to step in and do for this woman's arm what he himself could not do.

That night as he wearily climbed aboard the mission boat,

Messenger II, he had a heavy heart. After a simple meal in the small cabin of the boat, he looked directly at Percy Wills and announced, *"Percy, this is the place God wants me to be."*

Young Indian women were dying in childbirth; men were suffering bone injuries in logging accidents; children were dying of diseases that could be successfully treated. The needs were vast.

Herman Alexander McLean had married Hester Marion Card in

Dr. McLean at Bella Coola

1924. In 1928 he graduated with a doctorate of medicine from the University of Manitoba. After graduation, he worked for one year in Togo, Saskatchewan, and then moved to Bella Coola, British Columbia. The McLeans loved the people, the Indian people especially. Dr. McLean often travelled into the interior of the region towards Williams Lake. For three or four days he and his nurses would set up camp with makeshift tents. The Anaheim Indian people came out of the hills on horseback for medical help.

During their seven years at Bella Coola a sense of unrest began to rise in their hearts. In his years as a university student, Dr. McLean had been deeply moved while reading about the life of the great missionary David Livingstone. Dr. McLean wrote, "During the winter of 1918, while still in medical school, I started attending missionary meetings. I became deeply interested in missions. I prayed daily, asking the Lord if He wanted me to become a missionary. After reading the life of David Livingstone, my desire to be a missionary increased greatly. That man died while on his knees praying. What an example!"

The McLeans felt that they were to prepare for missionary work in Africa. They communicated with a mission in Kenya, and set their hearts to care for the Masai people. In preparation Mrs. McLean left her four children with close friends, and attended Normal School [teachers college] in Vancouver to upgrade her teaching credentials.

In the fall of 1935 the doctor felt he needed Bible School training, so the family moved to Three Hills, Alberta, to study at Prairie Bible Institute. While there, the disappointing news came to them that the application to Kenya had been refused.

They applied to the African Inland Mission and were again turned down. *Not without hope*, they were still to discover the place God wanted them to be. So they applied to another mission, the Sudan Interior Mission and, for the third time, were not accepted.

"One morning in my devotions," the doctor wrote, "I was deeply stirred by those words in Ezekiel 3:4, 'Son of man, I have called you not to people of strange speech and hard language, but to a language you know.' This seemed to tell me that I was to be a missionary in my own country, but because I so admired David Livingstone I had firmly set my mind on Africa."

As the doors to Africa seemed barred to him, he prayed one night in a public prayer meeting at Three Hills, "Oh Lord, I'll go to the toughest place on the West Coast if that is what you want." Completing Bible School studies in April, Dr. McLean went to Vancouver to take post-graduate studies in surgery and medicine at Vancouver General Hospital.

On April 28, 1937, he received a wire from Percy Wills. It

read, "The Shantymen's Christian Association is having its annual meeting in Victoria on April 30. Could you come be with
us?" Dr. McLean later stated, "I was surprised to get that letter;
in fact I was shocked. I had never heard of the Shantymen. I
had no idea who Percy Wills was; I had never been to Victoria;
I had no money. I decided I would go if God was in it. If He
was, then He needed to provide the money for transportation.

"The next evening, April 29, as I was leaving the hospital,
three Hindu men approached me and asked if I could direct
them to a dying man. They asked if I could help them draw up
his will in English. After the job was done they asked whether I
smoked. I told them that I didn't. They said, 'Well, you can use
the money any way you like.' One of the men stuffed a roll of
bills into the pocket of my white coat. I praised the God of
Heaven and returned to my room walking on air. I was to meet
Percy in Victoria and find out what the Shantymen Christian
Association was all about."

In Victoria, Percy took Dr. McLean to a Shantymen's prayer
group gathered at the Y.W.C.A. He was delighted to meet these
people. He wrote, "What a joy filled my heart. It was just a little
taste of heaven. Sweeter fellowship I have never enjoyed before. I felt such a sense of God's presence as those people
prayed. They prayed with such a deep burden for the needs of
the people of the West Coast. It made a lasting impression on
me."

At the end of the day Percy asked him if he would like to
make a trip up the West Coast. The medical needs were enormous and there was no doctor or hospital between Port Alberni
and Port Alice, a distance of two hundred miles.

When Percy and Dr. McLean boarded the boat, the doctor
was perplexed. There was no food, no gas, no cash, no medical supplies. When asked if he had instruments, he replied,
"Well of course not; all my things are back at Three Hills."

Percy told him that the Shantymen lived in total dependence
on God. This was just talk to him; he had never experienced

this kind of living before. Percy said, "Doc, we'll kneel down here by the bunk and ask God for everything we need." Percy prayed and laid out before God all their needs. By noon they had everything they needed. The Red Cross had given the "Doc" $150 worth of supplies and equipment.

Messenger II in Victoria Harbour, 1940

When he returned to the boat with boxes full of things, Percy told him to look in the cupboards. There was food—and lots of it. The gas tanks were full. Dr. McLean recalls, "We had everything we needed and were able to leave on schedule at 1:00 p.m. that Monday afternoon."

The West Coast of Vancouver Island is called the "Graveyard of the Pacific". The rugged coastline has rock-face mountains descending into the depths of the sea. Shallow water and jagged rocks make navigation treacherous. Sudden winds and off-shore storms disturb the waters all too frequently. Seldom are there calm and peaceful seas.

Two months after leaving Victoria on the *Messenger II*, Percy Wills and Dr. McLean arrived at the cannery in Nootka. It was July 10 and they had already treated hundreds of cases of illness and injury.

That day at Hecate, when the woman with the injured elbow had travelled six hours for help, the doctor knew beyond doubt that God wanted him to establish a hospital in Nootka Sound.

Percy thanked God that this doctor had the courage to trust God and tackle this challenging mission.

Dr. McLean had received a good wage during his years of practising medicine. He had a nice home for his wife and family as well as a car. He frequently questioned Percy about how he would support a wife and family with no known income. Percy assured him that God had supplied all his own needs. Frequently his faith had been tested but he could not name one time that God had let him down. This was difficult for the doctor to understand, but during those two months, he had seen the simple evidence of the total supply of needs met—and he couldn't argue with that.

When they left Victoria, Percy produced a little Oxo box. He said, "Doc, this is our bank." Dr. McLean later said that, "whenever we had a need, Percy would send me to that little box to get the cash. Many times I would empty it completely. A day or

Nuu-chah-nulth children

so later, he would need something and he would send me again. I would find it full again. God really looked after that little Oxo box."

Was it possible to believe that, because an Oxo box could be filled with change for two months, the same God could build a hospital in the remoteness of Nootka Sound?

Aerial view of Esperanza, circa 1966

CHAPTER 2

OXO

box

faith

K neeling beside their bunks aboard the *Messenger II* that summer of 1937 was not unusual for Dr. McLean and Percy Wills. With a heavy heart, yet inspired by Percy's faith and the evidence of the continual supply of their needs (and a never-empty Oxo box), Dr. McLean resigned himself to prayer and not to reason. Two men in their forties, with families in Victoria, asked God to provide a hospital for the people of Nootka Sound.

As was their custom, they prayed in a rather business-like manner. They reminded the Lord of every detail they could list regarding the materials that would be necessary for the construction. When they finished, being men of action, one said to the other, "Well, let's get busy. Let's not sit around here waiting for everything to drop down from the sky."

At McBride Bay, located on Hecate Channel in Nootka Island, was a small sawmill. The manager of the mill probably could not have prepared himself for these two men even if he had days of prior notice. Boldness and good humor characterized their every action, and such a pair was probably overwhelming, even to a tough man of the woods.

Percy simply said, "We have come to ask you the cost of lumber for a structure 14 feet by 32 feet, for the purpose of building a mission hospital." The manager answered abruptly, "I'm not interested in mission hospitals!" and turned to walk away. Percy called after him, "I didn't ask whether you were interested in mission hospitals, I asked for the price of the lumber." The manager replied gruffly, "Come back in half an hour and I will tell you."

When they returned, the manager was nowhere in sight. The pair went into the office to see if he was there. The bookkeeper grinned and said, "Take as much lumber as you want. It won't cost you a penny." A couple of sawmill workers offered to help load the lumber on board and two very happy men set out for Esperanza. A stream with fresh mountain water flowed onto the rocky beach, and the men trusted that it would be an endless supply of water for the demanding use of a hospital.

Esperanza was the spot where the doctor felt he should establish a base to care for the needs of the people in the area. The

McBride Bay, circa 1935

Tahsis, circa 1934

Nuu-chah-nulths had frequently camped on this narrow shelf of land for a time of rest and reflection. To them it was TLAWE MUXTSOO.

A canopy of giant firs, cedars and alders shut out the light overhead, and a dense tangle of fallen trees and undergrowth made penetration almost impossible. Near the water's edge the afternoon sunlight encouraged salal, thimble and salmon berries which flourished in abundance. A narrow ribbon of beach allowed for favorable boat landing and, when the tide fell, the beach broadened into a picturesque, boulder-strewn shore.

Clearing began. Dr. McLean, having been raised on a farm, understood hard work. From dawn till dusk the two men worked. Many people were unsure that Dr. McLean was really a medical doctor, simply because they doubted that a man with such education could also use an axe and a machete with such skill and diligence.

By the end of summer enough ground was cleared for the building to be constructed. Local men from the logging camps and canneries came to assist. To all those who enquired, Dr. McLean announced that he expected to open the hospital by November 1 of that year. Percy left for Victoria at the end of August, leaving the doctor alone. He actively sought a lawyer and began to work on the legal arrangements for establishing a hospital.

During this time the doctor continued his medical work in an office supplied by the Canadian Packing Company at Hecate, about a mile across the inlet.

He recalls, "Just after supper one night I left Esperanza for Hecate to pack my gear for the transfer to Esperanza. I hadn't noticed that a storm had made up and, after I pulled away from the shore, I realized I was being carried onto the rocks by the strong winds and tidal currents. It was dark and I had to struggle to get the little boat turned around and headed back.

"When I was almost at the shore of the hospital, a bright light lit up the whole area. It was a spotlight from a boat. I hadn't heard it because of the noise of the wind. As it came closer, I heard someone calling for a doctor. I answered them and they shouted over the wind, saying, 'We have a sick man aboard.' We beached our boats and tied them securely to a log. The men lifted their sick friend from the boat and carried him to the little hospital. It was plain to see that he was in bad shape and needed surgery immediately.

"I had anaesthetic and instruments but needing someone to help, I said, 'One of you fellas will have to give the anaesthetic to your chum.' They all

Patients arriving at the first hospital.

took for the door. Finally the youngest of the lot said he would help.

"I put on my headlight and gave directions to my new recruit. In a few minutes the surgery was over and the patient was on his way to recovery. By 11:00 p.m. the patient was awake and free from pain."

The date was November 1, 1937, and the hospital had opened for business.

Dr. and Mrs. McLean

CHAPTER 3

Mrs. McLean wanted to go to Africa

*I*t was a puzzle to Mrs. McLean. Her husband's prayer was being answered, yet neither her thoughts nor her heart leaned in this new direction.

Many times she pondered, "How did that Shantyman missionary Percy Wills ever hear about the doctor's prayer?" Percy had been in Victoria and Dr. McLean had said his prayer in the presence of a small group at Prairie Bible Institute in Three Hills, Alberta.

"I will never forget that prayer," she said later. "I dearly wanted to be a missionary in Africa. All my preparation had been with an intent to serve the Masai people in Kenya. I didn't want to go anywhere else and that was as plain as could be to me. But at that prayer meeting my husband prayed, 'Lord, if you want to send me to the toughest place on the West Coast, that's fine by me. I do want to go to a difficult spot.' "

Mrs. McLean did not agree with that prayer. She did not even say Amen! Instead she said to herself, "Wait till we get home; I will get him!" When they got home, she confronted him, grasped the lapels of his coat and, looking sternly into his eyes, said,

"What in the world made you pray a prayer such as you prayed tonight?"

After hearing of the doctor's delight in meeting Percy and of becoming acquainted with the faithful Shantymen's prayer group in Victoria, her mind and heart were still not lightened.

Later, when the letter of invitation came for them to become involved full-time on that desolate coast of Vancouver Island, she was not interested at all. "I reacted strongly to that letter and I told my husband, 'I don't want to read it!' " She never did read that letter.

Percy's request for the doctor to make the West Coast trip in May had seemed urgent. The doctor faced not only financial responsibilities for a growing family but also was in great turmoil as he considered his wife's feelings about this new mission endeavor. With a heavy heart for his family and a strong, irrepressible desire to preach the Gospel, he again prayed. On his knees, as was his custom, he bared his heart to God: "Lord, my family is at Three Hills. As soon as school is out they will need a place to live. If you are expecting me to stay in British Columbia, you had better supply us with a home—and I hope you will do it fast."

Nootka Cannery, circa 1928

In less than four hours after that prayer was uttered a phone call came to the Wills' home. A family in Sidney wanted someone to live in their home while they were away for several months. Percy and the doctor went immediately to look at the place and were delighted to find it large enough for the McLean family of four children (with one more expected in July). The doctor felt a sense of reassurance flood his spirit as he realized that every circumstance was somehow being cared for.

In July 1937, about the time Dr. McLean felt deeply the need for a hospital in Nootka Sound, Mrs. McLean gave birth to a son, Garth. He was a brother to Max, Donnel, Shirley and Bruce.

Friends and relatives gathered around this 32-year-old mother with her five children to support and help her. Relatives wanted to protect her. Concerned friends counseled her to remain in Sidney, saying, "There are no schools and there are no churches; it is absurd to take your children to a place like that." They added that the isolation would be unfair for the children, and their development would be greatly hindered. Her own doubts and the words of her caring friends caused her deep anguish and confusion.

Near the day that Garth was born her husband was aboard the *Messenger II*. It was at this time, weary from the long hours of caring for the sick, that Dr. McLean told Percy he felt Nootka Sound was to be the location for a hospital. When Mrs. McLean received word that her husband felt they were to be missionaries on the West Coast of Vancouver Island, tears slipped from her eyes. She prayed for a willing heart to be obedient in this difficult decision. Great sorrow overwhelmed her and remained with her all the rest of her life; but with it came a flood of peace—the peace of God that reassured her that He would neither leave her nor forsake her.

In September, along with her five children and their belongings (including British Columbia correspondence courses for the three older children), Mrs. McLean boarded the S.S. *Princess Maquinna* in Victoria. It was midnight and the air was clear and crisp. The children were excited and their mother was tired, yet calm and peaceful. A number of friends from the Shantymen's prayer group helped her load her possessions aboard. On the dock before boarding, loving arms hugged each one and tears flowed freely. Prayer was offered for safety on the journey and for courage to face the unknown. The final whistle blew; it was time to depart. The agony of separation stabbed Mrs. McLean's heart like a sharp knife as the gang plank was pulled aboard. The family stood at the railing as the Maquinna moved astern. Their friends on the dock began to sing,

> *"Take the name of Jesus with you,*
> *Child of sorrow, and of woe.*
> *It will joy and comfort give you,*
> *Take it then where'er you go."*

The lights of Victoria gradually faded away and the family felt alone. The unknown was as dark as the waters they saw beneath them. The steamer gathered way and the midnight chill chased them to their cabin and bunks below.

Two days later, they arrived at Nootka where a large cannery was operating. Beyond the dock was a five-story hotel and many comfortable-looking homes snuggled against the hillside. One of the hotel staff came aboard and inquired whether Mrs. McLean was on the ship.

"I have a message from your husband," he said. Her heart sank for a moment. But the young man continued, "You will have to get off here and stay at the hotel. A place is not ready for you at Esperanza." With those words, Mrs. McLean struggled with her emotions, wondering, "What in the world will I do in a hotel with five children?"

The warm days of September faded as the cool ocean mists of October and low overcast skies settled around the cannery. Mr. Lutz, the hotel owner, was very kind. The family was accommodated in a large upstairs room, and laundry and kitchen facilities were made available.

The older children enjoyed Nootka. Eight-year-old Shirley became a shadow of "Mrs. Jumbo", an Indian lady who cleaned for the hotel. Shirley called her Grandma.

The stories the fishermen told around the big hotel fireplace at night were intriguing. With a wide-eyed, captivated audience, the fishermen related their fish stories and experiences at sea with sensation and melodrama. By day, the three older children enjoyed watching the boats off-load their massive catches ashore for processing.

Max, eleven, and Don, ten, were given a job keeping a boat pumped out. They faithfully attended to this each day. One day, after a downpour, the docks were treacherously slippery. As Max was about to jump into their boat to pump it out, he slipped and plunged into the icy-cold water. Don was unable to reach him and Max was unable to get to the dock and grab something. Distressed, Don began to shout for someone to come and help. Some Indian men heard the calls and rushed to the scene as Max was going down for the third time. One of the men grabbed a pike pole and caught Max by the seat of the pants. He was

Hotel at Nootka Cannery where Mrs. McLean and her five children lived for almost three months in 1937.

unconscious when they pulled him out but the men knew how to treat him. Don watched in horror as Max lay limp at the entrance to the hotel. He was certain his brother was dead but it was not long until he regained consciousness and opened his eyes. He soon revived, jumped up and was ready to go again.

Mrs. McLean was kept busy inside the hotel with the youngest boys. Bruce, six, was active and needed watching. Garth was the baby. He had been extremely ill just a few weeks before leaving Sidney. When Percy, who had returned to Victoria, heard of the serious condition of the baby, he had rushed to Sidney and gathered the family for prayer. Miraculously, Garth was healed and restored to health. He was a good baby.

Many hearts of the fishermen and cannery workers were softened as his mother bathed him every morning in a tub placed on one of the dining room tables. Then, of course, the laundry for a baby and four active older children was no small task.

After two months, a fisherman brought a message from the doctor to his family: "Come to Esperanza on the next boat that will bring you. I have a place ready and I can't wait much longer to see you."

On November 4, just four days after the first surgery was performed at the little Esperanza hospital, the doctor's family climbed aboard a fish packer and completed the last leg of the journey to their new home.

Dr. McLean had been gone for seven months. He had not yet met his new little son. His heart was torn knowing the pain, the inconvenience and the struggles his dear wife was suffering. All he had ready was a little shack. He knew it was inadequate but he hoped that she would be willing to work alongside him.

The fish packer seemed to travel far too slowly. As the vessel turned from Tahsis Narrows into the opening of Hecate channel, the skipper said, "We will soon be there now." The children excitedly scanned the shorelines on both sides of the channel, competing to be the first to see the new hospital with their dad waving at them from the shore. Finally, the motor slowed. "This

The McLean Family, 1938
Standing (L to R) Don, Marion McLean, Max, Dr. Herman McLean
In front (L to R) Garth, Shirley, Bruce

is Esperanza," the skipper announced. For a moment the family was hushed. All they could see were two small shacks. Their most imaginative dreams could not have helped them foresee such a dismal scene. Surrounding the shacks was dense under-brush; towering above the underbrush were enormous fir and hemlock trees; and close behind were steep, rock-faced mountains.

As Mrs. McLean climbed out of the skiff with the baby in her arms and put her feet on the soil at Esperanza, a twinge of sorrow touched her heart. She stood there feeling very much alone but at that same moment, she began a new chapter in her life of prayer, asking God to help her during that day and in the rest of the days that she and her family would be serving Him at Esperanza. Mercifully, she was unaware of the hard work, the sorrows, the loneliness and misunderstandings that, in the days ahead, would send her to her place of prayer in order to find strength and courage to continue with the tasks of her life.

"I will never forget that first month we were there," she said. "It rained and it rained. I had never seen so much rain in all my life. The roofs in the buildings were leaking; the window frames were leaking; everything was leaking. Water was also rising under the foundations of the buildings. The wash tubs hanging on nails on the outside wall were banging with the force of the wind. I looked out the window at the storm in utter dismay. I didn't know what to do; I was at my wit's end. And then it dawned on me — my husband's prayer. When he had asked God to put him in a difficult spot, this was it! I believed that very minute that God had answered his prayer. I was able to relax a bit after that and somehow made it through the day."

One of the little shacks was the hospital. It measured 18 feet by 36 feet and had three rooms. The other shack was the McLean home and was similar in size and architecture. Two nurses had heard of the new hospital and arrived on the

Princess Maquinna offering to help if they could. Of course, they were needed and greatly appreciated.

The hospital became a busy place. Numerous accident cases were brought from various logging camps and neighboring villages. Maternity cases and all sorts of other medical conditions arrived for treatment.

"In those days everybody had to help," Mrs. McLean recalled. "Whatever the need was we had to be there and measure up." The doctor was precise and very exacting, especially with fractures. He called the shots in no uncertain terms. "Sometimes it wasn't easy to 'measure up'," she said with a chuckle.

There was no end of laundry. All the water had to be carried from the nearby creek and the laundry was done by hand with a scrub board. Cooking, cleaning and caring for the children occupied her days and the time went fast. Mrs. McLean did all the meal preparation and also entertained or comforted loved ones who had accompanied patients for medical help. The nurses and a male worker ate with the McLean's and shared the small living room.

Besides the two preschoolers, she had three children to supervise in correspondence courses. A lean-to was erected along the north side of the McLean shack. It served as a bedroom by night and as a classroom by day. Cold and dark, it was not at all conducive to study. Furthermore, there was really no time for Mrs. McLean to help the children with their work. Since she had been a teacher however, she was persistent and they were able to complete a part of their required curriculum that winter.

For nine years that little shack was her home. She was a gifted homemaker but the strain and confinement were hard. She did the best she could for her children. Daily she humbled herself before the God whom she dearly loved, asking for a willing heart to work with her husband amongst the urgent medical and spiritual needs of the West Coast people.

Mrs. McLean was very much a lady. She also possessed a great sense of humor and spirit of adventure—essential ingredients that helped carry her through those first few difficult years.

The S.S. *Princess Maquinna.*
Served 40 communities on the west coast of
Vancouver Island from 1913 to 1952.

CHAPTER 4

A larger hospital had to be built

*T*he little shack with three rooms soon proved too small for the number of patients needing treatment. The doctor prayed, asking God to somehow provide a larger building for the sick.

One night he dreamed he was gathering money. Numerous bills were within arm's length; all he had to do was reach out and get them. He dreamed he had accumulated $1,000. It was the winter of 1937-38, and Canada was suffering from the Great Depression.

Mail came every ten days on the S. S. *Princess Maquinna*, via the post office at Ceepeecee (about a mile further up the inlet). Soon after his dream Dr. McLean received word from Percy in Victoria that he must come as soon as possible. As soon as he was free to go, he boarded the *Maquinna* and sailed south to meet his good friend once again.

While there, he had occasion to relate the needs of the hospital mission to his Shantymen friends. The impact was so great that individuals donated generously to help the doctor in his work. On the final evening of his visit he sat down to count

New hospital under construction, 1939

the donations. He was delighted to find the total amount added up to $1,000.

With a full yet humble heart he returned to Esperanza, rejoicing and praising God. As well as the $1,000, he also had in his possession a row boat, a small X-ray machine, and tools for the construction work.

In July of 1938 a second floor was added to the hospital "shack" thus providing beds for eight patients. One of the new rooms was a much-needed operating room.

By the following year it was evident that even the eight-bed hospital was inadequate for the number of patients needing hospital care. Dr. McLean had great doubts about whether it would be wise to undertake another construction endeavor so soon.

He wrote in February 1940, "You will remember, at our last annual meeting, we had many misgivings as to whether we should consider a new hospital." At the time, it should be noted that the Port Tahsis mill in McBride Bay had ceased to operate; the fishing had closed for the season; the largest logging camp had closed and other logging camps were considering closing. In addition, a hospital had been built at Zeballos for the gold mine workers.

"We were greatly perplexed but, when all matters are committed to the Lord, He gives peace." The doctor continued, "We prayed for definite guidance in the matters of a new hospital. At the time, we were crowded to capacity and something had to be done."

A letter came from the Shantymen headquarters in Toronto

and, with it, a promise of $4,000 designated for a new hospital. "This, of course," he wrote, "was our answer and we went forward. The new hospital has now been in operation for six months, and over one hundred and fifty patients have been treated."

The new hospital opened on August 6, 1939. It could accommodate sixteen patients. There were two, two-bed wards on the main floor as well as a large sitting room which was also used as a chapel. An X-ray room was established on the main floor. A unique, hand-operated elevator was installed for transporting stretcher patients from the first to the second floor. The kitchen was separated from the spacious dining room by a small hall.

On the second floor was the nursery, the doctor's office, a dispensary for medicines and hospital supplies, and a bright and sunny operating room. There was an emergency room as

First hospital building on left, addition on the right

The Hospital — 1948

well as three, two-bed wards. Later, additions were constructed to provide a six-bed men's ward and a new office.

During the opening ceremonies with guests attending from the surrounding communities, uncontrolled tears welled up in the doctor's eyes as he announced that the building was completely paid for. In two years, not only had he and his staff cared for many people, they had labored to meet the growing demand for medical help and, as well, had constructed three buildings.

The doctor was feeling encouraged in 1941 when he wrote, "We had no deaths this year. Many patients who arrived seemed like hopeless cases but every one of them got well and they went home. Praise be to God!"

❧❀❧

Dr. and Mrs. McLean would never take any acclaim for the construction of the buildings nor would they allow any credit to be conferred on them for planning, organizing or completing the projects.

The purpose of the mission was stated in the motto: "To Preach Christ and Heal Diseases." From the very beginning the doctor, and those who wished to join him, gathered at 6:00 a.m. for an hour of prayer. At breakfast hymns were sung, and after each meal a devotional was given. Patients who were well enough joined the staff in the dining room.

The staff's deepest desire, besides seeing patients restored physically, was to see them helped spiritually.

※※※※

The hospital was always busy as patients came by boat or airplane for the dedicated and experienced services of Dr. McLean and his staff. Should he have built the hospital in Africa? Or was he in the centre of God's will, caring for the medical needs of the people of the West Coast of Vancouver Island?

Lou Manning with winch, 1953

Clearing land at Esperanza 1940

Horse pack train, Zeballos Mine, circa 1920

CHAPTER 5

There was

no time

for play

*T*he first November at Esperanza made a considerable impact on the lives of Max, Don and Shirley. Perhaps they did not feel they were at their "wit's end corner," but they did feel they were at some distant corner of the universe. A storm during that first month was recorded as the worst in twenty-five years. Huge trees were toppled like match sticks, and branches were driven into the earth like giant arrows. The family thought the little shacks that were the hospital and their home were going to float away in the unusually high tidal waters.

There were many adjustments to make. There was no time for childhood play anymore. Neither were there any other children to play with. There was only endless work to be done. Life at Esperanza was a real trial and the children did not enjoy it.

A young man named Harold Shannon came to assist with the maintenance work but was unable to do it all, so the children were required to help. There was water to carry, wood to chop, dishes to wash, supplies to transport, and land to clear.

In addition, there were correspondence courses to be attended to, and the cold, dark lean-to beside the McLean house was not exactly the kind of classroom to which they had become accustomed. Due to the heavy demands on their time, the children were unable to complete the required curriculum material in one year.

Every ten days the hospital supplies came on the S.S. *Princess Maquinna.* During those first few years there was only one rowboat. Often, during the winter, the winds would be blowing with gale force. The two boys had the responsibility of rowing the mile to Ceepeecee where the supplies were dropped off at the dock.

They would load their little boat with food and mail and row the long mile back to Esperanza, sometimes in rough water. When they beached the boat, everything had to be carried to a shed where it could be protected from the rain. Sometimes they were able to use a wheelbarrow, but often they had to hoist heavy bags of flour, potatoes, and sugar onto their backs and almost crawl along, overburdened with the weight. The boys were 11 and 12 years old.

Shirley enjoyed helping in the hospital but she, too, had to work long hours. Perhaps her favorite assignment was serving

Ceepeecee, circa 1940

tea, coffee and other refreshments to the patients. She loved being on hand whenever an emergency came to the hospital. Her main job was applying analgesic balm and hot foments to patients who had sore muscles.

Meanwhile the clearing and building continued. The big limbs of trees had to be sawed off and disposed of. It was necessary to blast the roots and stumps from the ground, and the boys helped Harold with the BB winch and the dynamite.

Max and Don became skilled at swinging an axe and handling a bucksaw. From time to time loggers would come with their power saws and wedges and make blocks from the big logs on the beach. The boys could then cut and split these for firewood for the stoves. They supplied all the firewood required throughout that first winter.

Carrying water was an endless job. Every drop of water for the busy hospital had to be carried from the creek, bucket by bucket. All the water for laundry, cooking, cleaning and scrubbing required an almost continual bucket brigade. In the summer of 1938 two young men came to help. A 1,200-foot pipeline was installed to provide a continuous supply of water from the creek to the buildings.

The first day that water ran freely from the taps, the boys shouted and hollered, danced around and threw their hats into the air. It was cause for celebration. The ordeal of carrying water was over.

Ruth

Dorothea, Shirley and Lois

Shirley

Lois

Aboard the *Elizabeth*: Bruce and Garth seated on the wheelhouse, Don standing, and Shirley, Dr. and Mrs. McLean seated.

CHAPTER 6

The family

makes

a home

*F*ive years of pioneering went quickly. There was hardly
time to stop to evaluate all that had happened in those
years. During the school year 1941-42, the first of Mrs.
McLean's two years as a teacher in Zeballos, she realized she was
pregnant. The older children were delighted to welcome a charm-
ing little girl, Dorothea, into their family. She was born at Esperanza
and the doctor himself performed the delivery.

Three years later Lois was born, and the year following, baby
Ruth. That year the family moved into a lovely new two-story
home. Mrs. McLean worked hard to keep everything in her home
nice. Though there was an endless flow of visitors, and food was
often scarce, she had the knack of making something special out
of little.

The afternoon sun poured into the spacious kitchen. The
entire south and west walls had large picture windows providing
a breathtaking view of the channel. Boats of every kind, large
and small, were passing by at all hours. There were canoes, row
boats, speed boats, trollers, gill netters, seine boats, fish packers,

cargo ships, and tugs with log booms in tow—a never-ending source of interest and enjoyment.

But the greatest thrill of all to the family was the moment they looked out and saw the *Messenger II* nearing the dock.

Percy Wills

There were shouts of joy in the household and a "whoopie" as everyone climbed into boots and coats, hurrying to be the first to be enfolded in the strong welcoming arms of Percy Wills and his rugged shipmate/skipper, Harold Peters. The McLeans and staff also knew they had better have hot water for the *Messenger* crew so they could bath and have their clothes laundered!

A visit from these two was like a spring day after a cold dark winter. Their zest for life was contagious and their stories knew no bounds. It was like a constant celebration during their stay, and it was a sad day when they had to depart.

Harold Peters

Although some of the family did not like the sandwiches concocted by Percy and Harold, they would not refuse them nor miss the preparation of them for the world. Every time Percy and Harold came they brought the ingredients for their famous "Shantyman sandwich." Cutting big hunks of Mrs. McLean's home-made bread and spreading them generously with butter, the ritual had begun. Percy and Harold made everything so much fun. On one slice, one of them would spread mayonnaise while the other was expounding the attributes of the perfectly-shaped Spanish onion.

Percy would say, "You have cut that beautiful specimen just right, Skipper." Skipper would retort, "You tend to that mayonnaise there, Mate. You cannot get that on too thick or you will mess up the whole thing." The young people smiled with delight as these loving men nattered away so good-naturedly to each other. The sandwich was perfected as thin, juicy slices of an orange were carefully placed over the onion. The gourmet touch was the addition of peanut butter and sometimes lemon-seasoned salmon.

As the two men commented on their creation, delighted smiles would extend from one to the other. One would comment, "Oh, thank you, Lord, for making onions," and "Oh, thank you, Skipper, for slicing those onions just right," and "Thank you, Lord, that Shirley cried instead of me because she stood too close to the onions."

The McLean kitchen was the centre of much mission activity as well as family activity. Mrs. McLean often prepared special birthday celebrations for staff members. A birthday celebration included a special meal for the guest of honor and was followed by the traditional birthday cake.

The family loved doughnuts and pancakes. Dr. McLean was often involved in frying the delicious doughnuts that were often on hand for coffee time or evening snacks. One day the household ran out of doughnuts. Garth found that if he wanted a doughnut that day he would have to make them himself because all the other doughnut-makers in the house were too busy. Finding the recipe and wishing to make a generous quantity, he multiplied the ingredients a few times. When his mother came home in time to prepare supper, there were doughnuts everywhere—on the table, the counters, even the window sills . . . and Garth had not yet finished frying all his batter. Every dish had been used. Every corner of the kitchen displayed quantities of

Messenger II at anchor

doughnuts. Somehow they found enough containers for most of them and Mrs. McLean managed to have dinner ready by the time her family and guests arrived.

Garth and Dorothea were strong and healthy babies but Lois struggled for strength. Mrs. McLean became exhausted as, night after night, she rocked her sweet, fair-skinned, blue-eyed baby. A compassionate and kindly mother in Zeballos had heard of Lois's difficulty in gaining weight and strength. Her own baby son had been weaned for a week. When Ann Hill heard that Lois was not tolerating formula she asked the doctor if she might try to nurse Lois. The doctor and Mrs. McLean gratefully accepted her offer. Little Lois began to grow and gain weight as Ann lovingly nursed and cared for the hungry child.

After two weeks of Ann's care, a staff member, Margaret Manning, gave birth to a beautifully-formed baby but it did not breathe. It was stillborn. Ann and the McLeans talked this over and decided that Margaret might find comfort if she were to nurse and care for Lois. Mrs. Manning accepted, and she found solace as she held the baby in her arms and nursed her as she would have her own daughter.

With this new arrangement, the luxury of a good night's sleep brought renewed strength and energy to Mrs. McLean. She needed the extra strength, for she found she was pregnant with her eighth child. When Ruth was born, her eldest brother, Max, was 21.

Every mother experiences extreme anguish for her children at some time or another and Mrs. McLean was no exception. She often resorted to the power of prayer for help. Her prayer-life deepened and her dependence on a prayer-answering God created in her a beauty and a confidence that drew people to her. She was known to many who loved her as "Mummy McLean."

One weekend the doctor was in Kyuquot, a four-hour boat trip from Esperanza, when Mrs. McLean was awakened by whimpering cries from the bedroom of the little girls. She recognized that it was not a natural whimper; it was the cry of one who was sick. She hurried to the room to find that Lois was burning with fever. She wrapped the child warmly and carried her to the hospital, hoping that the night nurse could help her dispel the fever. Every attempt failed. The fever worsened and the small child became delirious. Neither the child's father nor any other medical help could be contacted until morning, when the radiophone communications opened. In the morning the nurse on duty phoned Kyuquot with a message for the doctor to call Esperanza.

When he heard the extent and duration of his daughter's fever, he became fearful that she would by this time have developed a brain condition that might be irreversible. (Antibiotics

Messenger II with some of hospital staff in 1943.
Centre — Harold Peters, Skipper, with hat in hand. Beside him Mrs. McLean and Dr. H.A. McLean. On deck of boat is Bruce McLean "R" and Garth. Donnel stands behind the women far "L"

were not on the market at this time.) There was very little else
the nurses could have done other than what they had already
done. He said, over the radio, "Please gather the staff together
and have them call on God and pray for my little Lois." With the
two other people who had gone with him to Kyuquot, he
dropped to his knees and they also prayed for Lois. God answered and Lois was healed.

Another time when Ruthie was four years old, she complained
of a very painful "tummy". Her symptoms indicated appendicitis
but she seemed so young for such a condition. By late afternoon,
Dr. McLean realized that he had to perform surgery on her tiny
body. It was a difficult decision. He called his nurses together
and asked them to hurry because her condition was becoming
alarmingly serious. Surgery was begun and her extremely-in-
flamed appendix was removed. His diagnosis had proved correct.

During this time the older children were leaving home for
further education. It was difficult to come to terms with the fact
that they would not be home for Christmas. Mrs. McLean would
miss them more than she could ever convey to them. She knew
that she could pray for each one and she spent many hours in
her prayers sending her love to her children across the miles.

McLean Home, 1964

CHAPTER 7

Family struggles of Growing Up

*M*ax found it very difficult to adjust to life in Esperanza. As a result of his time in Bella Coola, the year he spent at Three Hills, Alberta and the six months in Sidney, he had become very interested in sports, baseball in particular. He found it difficult to cope without his friends and without a regular classroom setting. Study by correspondence in restricted quarters was very trying. As the years passed, the conflict turned into intense unrest, creating a difficult situation for him at home. He felt he should be in a larger school where he could have lots of friends and enjoy the normal activities which boys his age were privileged to enjoy.

At age 15 he told his parents he was going to leave home, and he did. A staff member had come from the Nazarene School in Red Deer, Alberta, and suggested that Max go there. In Red Deer, he found the help he needed. He did well in school and participated in sports and other activities he had missed during the years of hard work at Esperanza.

Don, on the other hand, seemed able to accept the challenge of living in an isolated place; although, like Max, he did not necessarily enjoy all the hard work. He too would have loved to play sports like other boys his age and he would have dearly liked to have a friend, but he responded differently.

One summer, Don decided he would receive Jesus into his life. He loved the Scriptures. He took time to read the word of God every day and he always prayed on his knees. One time, as twenty or twenty-five people gathered at a service in the little church in Ceepeecee, a speaker challenged the group asking, "Is there anyone here to-night who would like to dedicate their entire life to serving God?" Don imme-diately stood to his feet and, in front of

Donnel

everyone said, "I would like to do that." This decision gave him strength for two more difficult years at Esperanza.

Shirley, who was eight when they first moved to Esperanza, also worked hard and did not really know what it was to play. She says, "I think I was twelve when I remember standing in the kitchen of the hospital racking my brain trying to figure out what to cook for the next meal." In those days the nurses wore crisp, starched linen uniforms. Shirley ironed most of those uniforms with a gas iron.

Fortunately for Shirley, she had a nature very much like her father's. If there was a job to do, "let's get it done" was her natural inclination. In her matter-of-fact way she pitched in to help wherever it was needed.

In 1938, the year after the hospital opened, a hotel was built on the property next door. It was a liquor outlet for the area. The presence of the hotel brought great anguish to the hearts of the mission residents, but to Shirley, the hotel brought a friend. The manager's daughter, Lola, was Shirley's age. Shirley was attracted to all that went on at the hotel but, of course, was forbidden to play cards and join in the dances.

She confesses that she did disobey occasionally. What growing girl can keep her feet still when music is so lively and inviting? She would complain to her friend Lola, "all I can do is go to prayer meetings." In later years she realized that it was those prayer meetings that gave her stability and discipline for her future life.

Max was gone. Bruce was growing and the question of education for the children was uppermost in the minds of Dr. and Mrs. McLean. They felt the children should be in a classroom with a full-time teacher.

Sunday nights, Dr. McLean then began to take Don, Shirley and Bruce the 9 miles by boat to Zeballos. In his sturdy old vehicle he drove them from the dock up the narrow mountain road to the school at the Privateer Mine. At noon on Friday, he picked them up for the return trip to Esperanza for the weekend.

They looked forward to the moment on Friday when their dad's car could be heard noisily climbing the mountain trail. Upon reaching Zeballos, they would head for his little office. There he would have some hot, homemade soup simmering on the stove awaiting their ravenous appetites. Often, a hearty pot of rice sat alongside the soup pot. The doctor made it extra inviting by sprinkling the rice with generous portions of cinnamon and brown sugar. The highlight of the week came as they helped the doctor tidy the office, pack his equipment, lock the office door and walk down toward the dock. It felt so good to be aboard the boat with their dad, knowing that they would soon be home. The familiar lights of Esperanza drained all the fatigue from their bodies. Home seemed so inviting and so secure. Mother's good cooking and the easy feeling of being home where laughter and love and friendship filled every room—these were the great joys in those difficult years of growing up.

Don was in grade 8, Shirley in grade 7 and Bruce in grade 3. Don by this time, was six feet tall, strong and husky. He was asked to do the janitor work for the school. This included keeping wood cut for the stove and keeping snow shovelled for a path. There were 16 students in the school and the young people appreciated their teacher.

Shirley recalls the cook stove they used in their quarters at Privateer. It was an oil stove and it was a real problem. "You could practically sit on it and never get burned." However, she loved to bake and the neighbors were kind enough to let her bake her bread and pies in their ovens. Why she ever baked pies or bread for the three of them she doesn't really know, except that she enjoyed it.

Bruce wasn't the easiest kid for Don and Shirley to look after but they did the best they could. When Shirley and Bruce would come out of the bedroom in the morning, Don would have the little wood stove in the living room crackling with warmth and while Shirley got breakfast ready, Don would head up the path to the school and build the fire in the wood stove of the classroom. When he returned, the three of them enjoyed breakfast, which usually consisted of oatmeal porridge dotted with butter and sprinkled with brown sugar.

Although Esperanza was home, the close community life was often awkward and uncomfortable for the growing teenagers. Dr. McLean had a simple trust in people and with the ever present shortage of staff, he would sometimes get a staff member who was not really an exemplary Christian.

Don tells of a man who was a "fantastic preacher." Don would sit spellbound, listening to him, gripped by his words. Working with him hauling freight and doing the other daily tasks and chores with him was however, a different story. "I never saw a man with a shorter temper. He would become absolutely furious and he didn't use language that was becoming of a preacher!"

"As teenagers, we were often falsely accused by some staff members. There were things going on in the community that were not Christian. I came to a point where I was going to make a decision; I was going to give up the faith.

"The devil was really working on me. He was tempting me to look at those staff members whose lives were just not right. We were living in such close quarters and working so hard that these examples loomed so large they posed a big problem to me.

"Over and over in my mind I would say, 'If this is Christianity, then I don't want it.' I was on the verge of throwing my desire to follow Christ overboard, I was struggling with such deep agony. Was I going to follow the Lord, or was I going to give it all up?

"Walking up and down a path in the woods, I was trying to sort things out. The anguish in my heart was so great. The Lord in His great mercy spoke to me as I walked. He said in His small, quiet voice, 'Don, don't look at the hypocrites. It doesn't matter where you are; there will always be counterfeits. Any church, any business, anywhere in the world, there will always be the counterfeit. Nevertheless, there is also the real. Don't focus on the counterfeit. That's not what you pattern yourself by. Think of those who are real. Think of the Christians that have meant something to your life. Think of those who have been changed by Christ. Think of those lives that radiate reality and truth. There is One to look at. Look at Him. Look at Christ.'

"Then, of course, I began to think of the dear ones who were precious, right there on the staff. Among them were my dear mom and dad, John Martens and Harold Shannon. Percy Wills allso came into my mind. That is when I made my decision to really follow the Lord. I would not to be stumbled by people."

In the school year of 1941–1942, Mrs. McLean taught school full time in Zeballos, the small gold mining town nine miles by boat from Esperanza. Shirley was in grade 8, Bruce was in grade 6 and Garth was just starting. Don and Max were attending high school in Alberta.

A float had been built at Esperanza near the shore for landing supplies and for easier access to the boats. However, in rain and storms it became slippery and hazardous. One Sunday evening, the group was assembled on the float ready to say good bye to the staff and climb into the boat to leave for another week in

Zeballos. Their gear included clean clothes and boxes with fresh supplies of food and school books. Unaware for the moment that the crowd and the gear had over balanced the float, they were all suddenly tipped into the cold, chilly water. With flailing arms and legs, mingled with screams of laughter and dismay, everyone safely maneuvered to shore but the school teacher and three of her students did not get to school for the next day.

Although there were diversions, the children increasingly felt the isolation and the loneliness. They would soon have to leave home to continue their education. Don was the first to go to Prairie High School in Three Hills, Alberta. Shirley went the following year. They both loved the school but it was a sacrifice for them and for their parents to have them gone from September through the end of June.

Shirley recalls, "When fall would come, I would stay awake nights dreading leaving home but when I got back to school, I would be happy there." The skipper on the *Maquinna* knew when it was time for Don and Shirley to board the boat for school. No matter what time of day or night it was, he would sound the horn as the ship passed by Esperanza. Shirley says, "We knew then that we had a day and a half to get ready. It took that long for the ship to get to Port Alice and back. On the way back, the skipper would sound the horn once again as he passed Esperanza for Ceepeecee (often it was in the middle of the night). With suitcases packed, we would dress hurriedly, load our things into the skiff and row to Ceepeecee." The Doctor always read Psalm 121 as a departing encouragement, then he would take them to the ship and wave them on their way for another school year.

In retrospect, Shirley remembers her youthful days at Esperanza with fondness and reverence. "Although we found it difficult at times we now know that we had many wonderful and valuable experiences there. We are thankful to God for what He taught us personally while at Esperanza, and we are most thankful for the life of faith and trust in God that was shown to us daily by our parents."

The quick way down from the school at Privateer Camp

BCARS 71381

Privateer Camp, Zeballos, circa 1933

Heavy sea crashes on TONQUIN Island driving immense spray more than 100 feet into the air.

CHAPTER 8

Bruce's
last
voyage

*B*ruce was fifteen and would soon face leaving home for high school. The little girls, Dorothea, Lois and Ruthie, were now six, three and two.

On September 17, 1948, Mrs. McLean, Shirley and Don, travelled by *Messenger II* with the doctor for Chamis Bay, Kyuquot and other points to preach and heal. It was a lovely day and the McLeans looked forward to a little trip with their two older children before they were to return to school.

Although Dr. McLean usually looked forward to these missionary tours, this one seemed to be different. "From the moment I started, there seemed to be a feeling of impending disaster. Although I did not relate it to my dear ones, I felt in my own heart it was going to be a costly affair—a cross to bear for the Lord. To avoid His cross was against my faith. I went forward, believing it to be His will—and feeling that death to us would mean life to others.

"During Saturday, Sunday and Monday we held services and visited the sick. Tuesday the weather looked bad and I suggested that Mrs. McLean and Shirley go home by plane. When they left,

I felt a good deal easier. My son, Don, was with me. Tuesday evening we felt obliged to move down the coast, ready for an early morning start— the best time for sea travel. It turned out to be a terrible storm! We lay anchored in a bay unknown to us (near what we later learned is called Rugged Point). Rugged it was! No sooner had we cast anchor than contrary winds began to drive us towards the rocky shore. We lay in our

Bruce McLean

bunks with dread. Then, lightning flashed across the sky and thunder and hail added to our fears. When morning came and we were safe, I fervently thanked God and headed back to safer waters.

"Wednesday the storm continued its wild fury and we held a service till well after midnight. Early Thursday morning, we set out again. We had reached about half-way home when conditions became so terrible I knew we could not make it. The water pump quit and we were forced to turn and let the wind drive us till we could get back to safety. By this time, my fears of impending danger were even greater. I decided to put the boat into the care of Mr. Bancroft in Chamis Bay and we took the plane home. The relief we experienced cannot be expressed as the float plane touched down near the hospital dock and we were greeted by our loved ones.

"Days went by while we waited for fine weather. The boat had to be brought back and it seemed that God was asking me to go and do it. I trembled every time I thought of it, for I was not a seaman but a farmer at heart. But, on Friday, October 1, the weather seemed ideal and the need for the *Messenger* was impressed upon me more and more. On October 2, my family had to go to Zeballos to see our Don off by plane for Bible School. That morning, my son, Bruce, said, 'Dad, let me go to Chamis Bay and help you with the boat.' I felt the need of company but feared to take him. The danger kept ringing in my heart. I tried to discourage his coming by saying, 'It costs too much, son.' Said he, 'I will pay the plane fare myself.' I did not want to be mean. He coaxed his mother, when I was getting my ticket in Zeballos, and I said to the agent, 'Give me one for Bruce.'

"In a short time we headed for the plane. Bruce was the happiest lad you ever saw. I was glad to have his company and help but felt uneasy and did not dare tell him what I feared. We left Chamis Bay at 12:45 p.m. and were soon in rough waters. The wind was howling and water was coming in the pilot house with every wave. Bruce became deathly ill and hung out of the cabin door for the next five hours. Once or twice I asked him to see if there was water in the bilge and he struggled below to have a look. He also tried to pump more gas into the fuel tank. I was busy trying to keep the little craft from turning over.

"Finally, about dark, and fifteen minutes from the entrance to the Esperanza Inlet, the engine coughed and quit. I turned to Bruce and said, 'Son, we have had it!' Madly, I looked for possible reasons for the engine stopping. To my utter amazement the gas line and the bilge were full of water! The flywheel had thrown water over batteries, wires, and generator. My hope lay in pumping the bilge. Three times the pump was disassembled and put together—only to end in disappointment! My heart was still not faint nor willing to give up. I then took up the floor boards and got the pump from its original place and tried to put

it near the flywheel where we could pump out water and allow
the engine to start. But the winds and waves tossed us about
until the wires were off the batteries and other parts were torn
away. Finally, the boat rolled and a floor board hit the distributor
cap, breaking it in two. Then I knew it was God's call—and we
prepared to answer; 'Here we are Lord! Have things Your own
way. If You want our lives, so be it, Lord!' Bruce, still ill, lay
down on his bunk. I put the skiff overboard; the wind took an
oar adrift! I said nothing, then I cast anchor, hoping it might
catch and hold us off the terrible reefs just a few hundred yards
away. The anchor held for a little, then let go, caught again, held
a little and then let go! I told Bruce there was no hope. We were
drifting slowly into the jaws of death. I scrambled for a pencil to
write my dear wife and family. Bruce asked me to put in a word
for him. We got matches prepared for keeping dry. We prayed to
God to have His perfect will. We both had no fear of death but
we greatly feared hurling, tossing waters, with boat and rocks
dashing us to bits. We lay in our bunks helplessly, praying and
waiting for the inevitable.

"Every fifteen minutes I peered through the door to estimate
how much longer it would be before we crashed against the
rocks. I helped Bruce into a lifebelt and he tried to persuade me
to put one on also.

"Finally—a crash!

"Lights off!"—and we knew that was it! Bruce jumped to the
cabin door. Lights came on for another second. I got to the door
and we clung together along the port side of the ship. Bruce
said, 'Let's stick together, Dad.' As we tried to get around the end
of the ship farthest from the reefs, a huge breaker took the craft
in the air and, without any good-byes, we went into the water
between the boat and the rocks!

"I swam . . . and swam . . . and swam . . . and held my breath.
My ears cracked! My lungs made peculiar noises. Water began to
get into my mouth. I feared I could not hold out another second,
then I hit the bottom of the boat! Just as I was going to take a

gulp of water that would have ended the scene, God sent me into the air. I saw a dark object and grabbed it! It was my boy, Bruce! He was already dead. Unable to speak, I let go, took another breath, and . . . into the billows again!

"Hurled against a rock, I grasped onto it, as only a dying man can. The waves went over me and drew me back. I took another breath . . . another wave . . . and I went onto another rock . . . and there I clung till the waters receded; then I was again dashed on the rock, only to be caught and almost swept away again. But God was my strength. The next withdrawal of the billows, I scrambled as best I could, right up the pinnacle of the rock (known as High Rock) before I would be caught by another wild

wave. There, safe at last in a cleft of the rock, I thanked God and felt I was either to be saved or die from exposure. I sat shivering on the sharp rocks, being drenched every five minutes or so with huge waves sweeping the rock and me.

"I asked God to keep the *Messenger* near. I would need food and clothing. I knew I could not last long otherwise. About six hours later, I saw another evidence of my God's power and purpose. He had lifted the ship over the rocks onto the shelf away from the storm. Oh, how I thanked God when I saw this!

October, 1948. The rock to which Dr. McLean tied himself when his boat foundered and his son drowned.

Messnger II up on the rocks

"When the tide fell and I could reach the ship, I got blankets and a few cans of food. I climbed back up the rocky peak and, covering myself with the wet blankets, decided to wait until God either saved me from the rocks or let me die of exposure.

"After two nights and a day (or more) thus exposed, my strained vision discerned smoke on the horizon. My eyes stared from their sockets. Was it possible that God was going to take me back to finish my job?

"The smoke was God's mercy ship! It was the Kyuquot Trollers Co-operative Association's vessel, *the Co-operator No. 10* (an appropriate name, under the circumstances) and, seeing my mad waving with a sheet, they altered course towards my hiding place. Rescued at last!

"Reaching the deck of the ship, I began to weep as a child. I was saved—perhaps for a purpose. Realizing that my work was not yet complete, I rejoiced. I felt as one who lives again!

"Upon returning home, I could not put into words what joy was mine. My thoughts were: 'Jesus is a Rock in a weary land, a Shelter in the time of storm.' Oh, that storm-tossed souls everywhere could seek and find a refuge in Him!

"The tragic loss of our son left us with deep scars. Perhaps he was the sacrifice we had to endure in order to carry out God's work."

Messenger II — another victim of The Graveyard of the Pacific. October 2, 1948.

CHAPTER 9

A
second
escape

*L*ess than forty-eight hours after the doctor had been rescued from the pinnacle of the rock, he felt it necessary to continue his office schedule in Tahsis and be on hand to care for his patients. The mission had only one small boat and it was in poor condition. Nevertheless, he went in it anyway.

When duties in Tahsis were completed and it was time to return to Esperanza, the engine would not start. A strong southeast wind was making up, indicating a storm but Dr. McLean knew it was important to return to Esperanza and be with his grieving wife. Concerned friends begged him to stay in Tahsis for the night but the doctor felt an urgency to get home. A seaworthy Tahsis company boat was made available and the manager himself offered to take him back to Esperanza.

It was getting dark. The wind was increasing, carrying sheets of rain. They headed out into the storm, thankful for a sturdy vessel under them. Not far down the channel the compass ceased to operate. That presented only a small problem since the spotlight could illuminate the shoreline sufficiently for adequate navigation. The manager knew the landmarks of the starboard shoreline.

Suddenly, midway down the channel and less than halfway home, the engine coughed and quit. The owner, with flashlight, quickly scrambled to discover the cause. The water was rough and the boat was tossing in the mounting waves. Without power the boat was being driven toward the rocky shoreline.

Above the noise of the wind and waves, the owner shouted to the doctor, "I have found the problem," a look of consternation on his face, "I put fifty gallons of gas in here yesterday. Someone must have stolen it."

Fortunately he had a spare five-gallon can of gas aboard but this presented another challenge. The efforts of pouring the gas from the container into the small opening of the tank proved to be next to impossible as the boat was tossed about by the wind and waves. In an awkward balancing act, the doctor held his hat over the tank, trying to prevent the wind from whipping the gas away while the other attempted to pour the gas.

They managed to get enough into the tank to get the engine started and slowly motored out into safer waters. Their immense sense of relief proved to be short-lived, however. There was another serious difficulty. The spotlight went out. No amount of tinkering could make it work. There was nothing they could do at this point except pray.

Meanwhile, Percy Wills and Harold Peters were in Clayoquot Sound when they heard of the death of Bruce and the loss of the *Messenger II*. (It should be noted that the *Messenger II* had been given to the Nootka Mission Association in 1947 when the sturdier vessel *Messenger III* had been built by the Shantymen's Christian Association.) They motored from Clayoquot Sound around Estevan Point to Esperanza as quickly as possible.

"We got to Esperanza in the afternoon," Skipper Peters recalls. "I think it would be the third or fourth day after the *Messenger II* had been wrecked. It was October and, by late afternoon, it started to get dark. The doctor had gone to Tahsis in some small boat. Mrs. McLean was worried and asked if we would go bring him home.

"When we got to the Tahsis Narrows, there was about a four foot-sea running and quite a wind blowing. We had not steamed past the marker light on the point more than five minutes when we caught sight of a light flashing over on the starboard shore near the beach. So we went over there to have a look. Here it was, a Tahsis man with Dr. McLean aboard."

Harold continues, "He was coming to Esperanza, bringing Dr. McLean. He had put gas in his tank the day before but somebody had pinched it and he had run out of gas. These two fellows were trying to pour the gas into the funnel and into the tank. The wind was blowing half of it away, I guess. So we went over and found them in this predicament. They were not very far from the beach. We hooked onto the boat and got the fellows aboard. They were soaking wet and nearly frozen by this time. We steamed on to Tahsis and secured the manager's boat at his float, before returning the doctor to Esperanza."

Left to Right:: (Standing) Max, Garth, Shirley, Don and Dorothea (Seated) Doctor and Mrs. McLean holding Lois and Ruth.

Church at Ceepeecee. Max George holding child near front.

Daniel Touchie, Samuel Touchie, Ken Mundy, David Haipie, Ernest Tutube, Phillip Mack (Percy Wills' Ucluelet guide when travelling by canoe), Lawrence Jack Jr.

Phillip Mack with grand niece Patty

CHAPTER 10

"With sincerity and a deep love for the people . . ."

Ceepeecee was a busy fish cannery and community of about 300 people. About a mile from Esperanza, it was first owned by the California Packing Company (C.P.C.) and later by the Canadian Fish Company.

Ceepeecee provided a large wharf for the ships and boats involved in the industry and it became the lifeline wharf for Esperanza. All supplies and equipment were dropped off there. The mail also was distributed from the Ceepeecee post office.

The majority of employees at the packing company were coastal Indian people. Their housing consisted of dwellings built on huge pilings driven into the rocky beach. Wooden sidewalks, firmly lashed and braced, separated one row of dwellings from the other.

The people at Ceepeecee were the first coastal Indians that Dr. and Mrs. McLean met. They liked Dr. McLean and helped him immeasurably in the first years of adjustment. They helped tremendously with the hard labor of building the three hospital buildings. The women from Ceepeecee helped Mrs. McLean with her duties as well. Some of the younger girls often babysat the three small McLean girls, freeing Mrs. McLean to help in some of the other areas of work.

Through the years, many helped in the ongoing work of the mission. James Adams, Joe Billy, Phillip John and Wilson Little worked on the construction of the hospital. Long hours of sacrificial service were rendered by George and Margaret August and their eldest daughter, Georgina, Earl and Helen George, Ernie and Julia Campbell, Agnes Brown, Florence Atleo, Roger and Violet Clarke, Allan and Julian George, Teresa and Gordon Louie, and others.

Dr. McLean preached in the Indian villages at every opportunity. The people were very polite and many attended his services to show their appreciation for his medical help, but their difficulty in understanding English was compounded by the fact that he spoke very quickly. With sincerity and deep love for the people, he earned a way into many of their hearts, and some welcomed the Gospel he was preaching.

Benny, Cora, and Peter Charlie. Good friends to the McLean children.

Among the Indian people, he found much sadness and grief. One man told the doctor that seven members of his family had died from drowning. Others lost entire families in fires. Tuberculosis claimed many lives. Alcohol abuse devastated the lives of both young and old. Young girls died giving birth. There were boating accidents. Agony and helplessness in these deaths gripped the hearts of Dr. and Mrs. McLean.

The villagers opened their

hearts to the staff as well and most people appreciated the fact that Dr. McLean and his staff genuinely wanted to help. In time, strong friendships and a mutual respect developed.

Many children were admitted to the hospital, and the nurses dearly loved these beautiful, chubby, round-faced children. Most of the illnesses were the usual childhood diseases, and ear, nose and throat problems. Some came with more serious problems and, sadly, did not survive.

The injuries resulting from alcohol abuse devastated relationships and ravaged homes. A young Indian mother was admitted to the hospital, having been severely and cruelly beaten by her husband when he was drunk. The nurses carefully tended her painful wounds and broken bones. As they did so, they prayed for her, knowing that her heart and spirit were also broken. They told her about Jesus and His love, assuring her that His love was unconditional. They told her that He accepted her just as she was. They told her that He was loving and kind.

As she talked and cried in despair and hopelessness, they conveyed to her that forgiveness and comfort comes from the heart of the Lord Jesus. It was difficult for her to understand that she needed to believe that the love and forgiveness of Jesus was for her, personally.

One day, she responded and prayed that God would help her and her family. She also prayed for forgiveness for herself and for her husband's cruel treatment of her. In spite of his abuse, she cared for him and was committed to him.

One day, as she was recovering, still swollen and bruised, a nurse passing by her door heard the sound of a man's voice coming from within. The nurse paused and listened in protective concern. She recognized the voice and knew it was the patient's husband.

He was speaking softly and with much emotion, saying, "Will you forgive me?" She did not answer. The nurse held back an impulse to move in and guard her convalescing patient, but, instead, stood quietly beside the door, continuing to listen.

Again she heard the plea, "Will you forgive me?"

Then quietly, with measured words, the reply came, "The nurses have told me how much God loves me. They told me that Jesus died for me and forgave me all my sins. If God could forgive me, for I'm as bad as you are, then I can forgive you for what you have done to me." The nurse quickly moved away, wiping a tear from her eye.

✦✧✦

In the early years of the hospital the most devastating disease among the Indian people was probably tuberculosis. Most patients with T.B. were sent to the sanitarium in Nanaimo. Many were there for a year, and some, much longer. Many died there.

One lady told of the dark feelings she had when the doctor told her she would be transferred to the T.B. hospital. In her weakness and despair, everything about her seemed lifeless and grey. Depression had set in and she did not want to mingle with the other patients. She was homesick and spent most of her time pining and longing for home.

One day, a friendly patient came to her room to talk to her. She told her that she understood how lonely and frightening it was to be in a T.B. hospital. Then she added, "I have found that, when I pray and ask God to help me, He does help." The patient appreciated the friendliness of the lady but did not understand how praying could make her feel better.

Everyday, the praying lady came to visit and spoke a few words about prayer and faith in God. "Bit by bit, I began to listen to her," the patient said.

"Then, one day, I decided to try to pray. I asked God to forgive me for feeling sorry for myself. I asked also if He could make me feel different inside. I was standing by the window when I prayed this prayer. Do you know what happened?" she asked with a sensitive smile. "I looked outside and was surprised to see how green the trees seemed to be. Then I looked up into the sky and I thought I had never seen such a beautiful blue color in all my life. Everything outside seemed bright and beautiful. I puzzled over this unusual experience of seeing the trees and sky having such vivid colors.

"Suddenly, I realized that the God, whom my visiting friend had been telling me about, had done something for me. He had answered my prayer. I was sure of it. As long as I had lived I had never noticed the world and its creation appearing so fresh and beautiful. The dark feelings were gone. I had become different inside. My time in the hospital was not so lonely and frightening after that."

George and Margaret August with daughters
Georgina, Marguerite and Josie

These friends worked with
Dr. and Mrs. McLean

Ernie & Julia Campbell
Ernie's mother, Mattie

James Adams

Nurses standing on hospital steps where stretcher cases could be taken directly to the operating room on the second floor.

Hospital Staff 1951

CHAPTER 11

Nurses came
with
sacrificial hearts

"We need to do a lot of praying but we need to do a lot more dying." These were the words that caught the eye of Miss Lou MacIntosh as she read a copy of the Nootka Mission Review in the infirmary at Prairie Bible Institute, Three Hills, Alberta, in the winter of 1943. These words were penned by Dr. McLean and so gripped the imagination of this efficient nurse that she sent an application to him and was accepted immediately.

"We arrived at Esperanza before sunset. I thought I had never seen such a beautiful place in all my life. It was June. The sun was shining. Mrs. Rhodes had the flower and vegetable gardens in prize-winning condition and the flowers were magnificent.

"Perhaps this beauty stood out because everything else seemed quite primitive. There were only three or four buildings on the grounds, some having been towed from closed logging camps. They seemed drab and small but the surroundings seemed very beautiful to me."

Arriving in June 1943, she relates: "I was deeply impressed that first morning in the operating room. After the patient had

Miss MacIntosh became known as "Miss Mac", until 12 years later when she was married. After which time she became known to all her friends as Mrs. Morrison.

been placed on the operating table, and just before starting the anaesthetic, we nurses stood with bowed heads while Dr. McLean led us in a simple prayer asking for God's presence and guidance. In that holy hush, all care and anxiety were dispelled and our hearts were quiet. What an atmosphere in which to work."

She became the matron of the Esperanza General Hospital and remained for 12 years. During these years, she was known as "Miss Mac". Her duties ended when a tall, handsome, retired widower, Wesley Morrison, came to the mission. With her smiling consent they were married in August 1956.

By that time, in addition to the running water, the hospital was wired for electricity; but did not have its own source of power. The Esperanza Hotel Management graciously supplied the hospital with power from dusk until 10:00 p.m. When power was needed for the washing machines or for surgery, the hotel kindly assisted by extending to the mission the needed electricity.

Later, when an X-ray machine was purchased, the hotel never once denied a request for help. The X-ray equipment was essential for accurate diagnoses of fractures or other conditions needing X-rays. Of course, there was payment for its use, but money cannot measure the help that was extended to the nurses and their patients (as well as the laundress and the doctor) with these hours of power for the building.

The doctor had office hours twice a week both in Tahsis and in Zeballos. He also made monthly visits to the Indian villages of Kyuquot, Friendly Cove, Queen's Cove, Nuchatlahts, sometimes Gold River and the numerous logging camps in the Sound. He was an energetic man and always made a home visit when he felt it necessary. Because of this, the nurses often had to make decisions on their own, since the small communities were without any form of radio contact. The nearest doctor was 90 miles away in Tofino and he, too, could be contacted only through the Vancouver radio-telephone system.

On one occasion when the doctor was gone, the Indian agent brought in the priest, Father Shane, from Nootka. Earlier, he had a foreign body in his eye which had been removed at Nootka, but the eye was extremely inflamed. The nurses applied compresses and gave him sulfathiosol (this was before there was penicillin).

The nurse could see that the patient was quite anxious. Miss Mac adds, "So was I." The inflammation continued for a day or two and did not seem to be improving. Further, the doctor was not expected back for several days. Miss Mac went to Mrs. McLean and together they prayed for some insight into what they should do for Father Shane.

No answer was received and Miss Mac returned to the hospital with a feeling of despair and inadequacy. Shortly afterward, she returned again to Mrs. McLean's home and, once again, they prayed. This time when she left she felt assured that somehow the Lord would undertake to help.

When she got back to the hospital, a thought came to her. She remembered that a year ago a patient had been admitted with a similar problem. The question arose in her mind: "Now what did we use for that patient that we have not been trying?" She says, "I found the chart. The ointment Dr. McLean had prescribed was atropine ophthalmic ointment. We applied that according to the directions given for the other patient. When the doctor returned two days later he pronounced the eye perfectly healed."

Miss Mac continues, "If the doctor was away, and we had done our best, he knew we had done our best. We appreciated that he never scolded us for not doing something better."

Sometimes expectant mothers came early when they knew weather conditions might prevent them getting to the hospital in time for the delivery. Once, a young Indian girl was waiting for her first child to be born. The doctor was going to be away overnight and checked her condition before he made the decision to leave. Since women are often in labor a good many hours with their first child, he felt safe in leaving at that time.

About 10:00 p.m. that night Doris Thomas, the night nurse, came to Miss Mac to announce that the girl was in labor. Miss Mac asked the girl when her labor had begun.

She said, "Oh, it started this morning."

With a professional tone, Miss Mac scolded, "Why didn't you tell the doctor?"

"I just thought it was a stomach ache," she said, rather sheepishly. But the stomach ache got worse. The two nurses cared for her during the night and at 8:00 a.m. the next day, a healthy baby was born.

That entire winter Miss Mac and Mrs. Thomas were the only

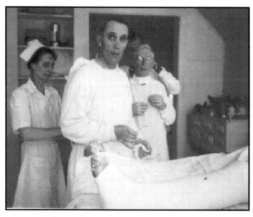

Miss Mac and Dr. McLean in the operating room

nurses at the hospital. Miss Mac worked the day shift and Mrs. Thomas worked the night shift. Not only did they have the nursing duties to attend to but they also had to do the cleaning. The floors had to be swept and washed and waxed. Often the doctor was seen sweeping the floor, willing to help wherever he could. The nurses felt badly when they saw him sharing the menial tasks but they greatly appreciated his help.

During surgery both nurses were needed. One morning a middle-aged patient was coming out of the anaesthetic following surgery. Miss Mac was sitting by his side monitoring his recovery. When he started to talk, she knew that he would soon be conscious. When his words became coherent, he began to say, with emphasis, "Oh, Miss Mac, I like you. Oh, Miss Mac, I like you. Oh, Miss Mac, I like you . . ." She was beginning to enjoy his amorous words until suddenly he changed his message, ". . . but I like Mrs. Thomas better."

"It was wonderful how the Lord looked after us," Miss Mac says wistfully. "Either help would come in a time of extremity or we were able to send the patient out if we were not equipped to handle the case. There were excellent First-Aid men in the Tahsis mill and in the other camps and they would help us in every way they could. I do not think a patient ever arrived at our hospital with a fracture or other condition that was not properly splinted and cared for. When they came with a patient and the patient needed to be sent to Vancouver immediately, they would help us get the patient ready for the plane."

One time, when the doctor was away, a patient came in with abdominal pain. Miss Mac suspected appendicitis. In those days there was a converted minesweeper owned by Gibsons Brothers which travelled between their two mills in Port Alberni and Tahsis. Miss Mac contacted Dr. Montieth in Tofino by radio phone. Dr. Montieth arrived the next day on Gibsons' boat, the M.V. *Machigonne.* He performed the surgery and left for Tofino on the return trip—ten hours in unfriendly waters.

On another occasion when the doctor was away, a woman was waiting to have a baby. The doctor felt certain she could not deliver the child normally. She would need a Caesarean section. By this time the hospital had purchased a double-sideband radio telephone.

The doctor faithfully called at certain scheduled times during the day. One night he made the radio call and was reassured that everything was in order and he did not need to make contact until next morning.

Shortly after his call the woman went into labor. As the hours slipped by, Miss Mac could see that no progress was being made. There was a practical nurse helping at that time. She was on duty that night. Miss Mac sensing the need for a second opinion consulted another staff registered nurse, and together they examined the weary patient.

The second opinion confirmed her fears. This lady was in difficulty. The lives of the mother and the baby were in danger. They had no other recourse in the middle of the night but to fall on their knees and pray, asking God, the Great Physician, to please come and help them.

Before they had finished praying the practical nurse came rushing to them and said that there had been a marked change in the patient. In a little over an hour, a healthy baby was delivered. Their prayers were answered.

Another difficult case was admitted with an eye injury. A man employed at the Tahsis mill had been treated by the First -Aid men before they brought him to the hospital. They had bandaged his eye extremely well, so Miss Mac had decided not to disturb the bandages. The doctor was expected home next day and she thought it best to leave the injury for him to assess. Later in the day the doctor phoned to say that he would be delayed a day or two more in Vancouver.

Next morning, Miss Mac found the man in exceeding discomfort. She proceeded to take the dressings off and found a small gash on his eyelid. The area around the eye was swollen and the flesh from the cut was protruding. She knew it had to be attended to. Finding the smallest curved needle and the finest available suture, she scrubbed, and donning sterile gloves she carefully sutured the injured eye. She says, "It healed surprisingly well."

Another time Doris Thomas triumphed in a case involving a

man who had come from the hotel one night in a state of drunkenness. He crawled into a vacant hospital bed with all his clothes on, including his muddy boots.

As she made her rounds to check her patients, she was startled at the presence of this self-admitted patient! He, too, was startled to see her and, in his senseless state, he jumped out of bed and chased her upstairs where the operating room was located. Her mind was racing as she wondered what she might do to bring him to his senses. Quickly she reached into the drawer where the

Edith Hungerford with two treasures

surgical supplies were kept and withdrew a cruel looking surgical knife with the scalpel blade in place. The intruder came stumbling into the O.R. after her. She wheeled around with her ugly weapon, threatening, menacing . . . the attacker fled down the stairs and out the door. She followed in determined pursuit as far as the door. He never returned.

<hr />

Many nurses assisted with the patient care at Esperanza. The first were Trissie Weller and Ruth Portway. They were followed by Hazel Benner, Hilda Richardson, Olga Bengay and Isabel Cameron.

Isabel Cameron specialized in surgical nursing. She and Miss Mac prepared an operating room procedure book, which was of great value to future nurses. Bundles for such things as maternity packs, abdominal surgeries, tonsillectomies and suturing were kept up to date and ready for immediate use. The night nurse used the largest size aluminum pressure cooker to sterilize the necessary bundles each night. Dr. McLean appreciated his competent surgical staff and performed numerous surgeries in all categories.

Miss Fanny Carlile followed Mrs. Morrison as matron and continued in that position for 16 years, until she retired in 1972. Beulah Harnum became matron until the hospital closed in 1973.

When Miss Carlile took over the responsibility as matron in 1956 the workload remained somewhat the same. Sometimes there was a good supply of nurses and sometimes there was a marked shortage.

The *Bruce McLean*

Conditions by this time were much improved. The mission had purchased a power plant and along with the electricity came running water which extended to every building. A never-ending supply of water and electricity complemented the efficiency of the hospital staff. So, by this time, pioneering days were mostly over but the long working hours were to continue until the hospital closed.

Miss Carlile came with a wealth of experience in nursing. She had been a missionary nurse with the United Church in small hospitals in northern Ontario and northern Saskatchewan. Prior to coming to the mission, she had been on staff at the Saskatoon Bible College. It was at this school that she heard about the mission and learned of its whereabouts.

Her introduction to Nootka Sound was somewhat eventful.

Before her nursing duties began, the doctor invited her and a friend on one of his regular house calls at the village of Friendly Cove. They enjoyed meeting the Indian people who were very kind and hospitable, as is their custom. The *Bruce McLean,* named after the son lost at sea, was anchored a fair distance out in the cove. Miss Carlile and her friend from Saskatoon managed to disembark from the boat into the skiff with no difficulty.

But after the visit, when it was time to climb from the skiff back onto the *Bruce* which was quietly rolling in the waves, it was a totally different story. One of the ladies, not knowing the proper procedure, and experiencing some difficulty with her calf-length skirt, stepped on the edge of the skiff which promptly capsized, throwing all four occupants into the icy waters. When Miss Carlile came up, with her characteristic good sense of humor, she remarked, "Praise the Lord, my glasses are still on my nose."

Since Miss Carlile's friend could not swim, the oarsmen and Miss Carlile had quite a time getting her aboard.

It looked like quite a spectacle from shore as the doctor and other crew members and villagers looked on. In such situations it is West Coast tradition to laugh and tell the soaking-wet individuals that they are now "true West-Coasters." Falling into the "chuck" happens to everyone at one time or another.

Miss Carlile found the Indian children to be her favorite patients. She dearly loved to feed them, nurture them, cuddle them and see them restored to health. One time she had as many as sixteen little ones to care for.

Children, whether they are sick or not, can be full of mischief. One day in the children's ward she saw a face cloth hanging above the window frame on the curtain rod. She wondered how on earth it got there. She beckoned to the little boy whose bed was closest to the window, saying, "Come here!"

He came and she asked, "Did you put that up there?" He replied impishly "Yes!" So she said, "Well, you just get up there and get it down." So he scampered up the curtain like a little monkey and brought it down. She often commented about him later, "He was the cutest little guy, and so full of mischief . . . ."

Miss Carlile did not enjoy caring for the men as much as she did for the women and children. Penicillin was the newest drug in her early days at Esperanza and most of the men received shots which proved to be extremely effective in preventing as well as healing infections. The men in the ward always knew when Miss Carlile was making her rounds to jab these poor helpless loggers with the potent medication. It was a job she was determined to finish quickly. The other nurses acknowledged that the men as well as Miss Carlile would rather not have to go through this procedure.

One day the superintendent of the Tahsis Mill was admitted to the hospital with a chest condition. There was no private room available for him so Miss Carlile had to put him in with five other men. Of course they all knew him and respected him highly. The doctor had written on the order sheet that he was to wear a pneumonia jacket—a heavy flannel sleeveless thing with one shoulder seam and ties to hold it together on the other shoulder and down the side. As Miss Carlile was taking it into his ward, the bell rang for her to quickly check a maternity case, so she left the jacket with him with the instructions, "Put this on. I will be back as soon as I can.

"When I came back," she relates, "He had put the thing over his pyjamas, and the strings were all tangled. He looked as if he was in some sort of a straight jacket." The patient from the next bed was ambulatory and was trying to help him. As the two struggled in vain to get the thing on, the other men, peeking from behind the curtains, were laughing uncontrollably at their fearless leader.

⚜

One morning, the doctor informed the nursing staff that one of the little boys in the ward was terminally ill and would not live very long. One of the nurses kept a flannel-graph board behind the piano and enjoyed telling Bible stories to the children in her spare time. One afternoon the nurse on duty found this sick child sitting on the couch crying. She asked him what was wrong. What was making him feel so bad?

He replied, "I want to hear more stories about Jesus." The nurses delighted in his love for Jesus. He could often be heard in his room singing the songs and choruses they had taught him. One morning, he begged the

Miss Carlile

doctor to let him go to the early morning singing and praying time with the staff. Permission was granted and he found great delight in worshipping the Lord that morning.

※◎※

Once a man was admitted who was dying. As the nurse examined his weakened condition, a heaviness and a sadness settled upon him. Later in the evening, she cautiously said to him, "Sir, my father died not long ago and I'm very comforted to know that he's in heaven." The man looked at her but said nothing.

The nurse continued to care for him in every way she could. He was fiercely independent, as many of the West Coast men were, and he stubbornly resisted the help and care that the nurse wished to give him.

His condition weakened quite rapidly. One evening when the burdened nurse went into his room he looked at her and folded his hands as if to pray. Feebly he asked, "Where is my rosary?" The nurse searched all his belongings but could not find it. Finally she sat down on the chair by his bed and said, "Maybe I can pray for you. Will you pray if I show you how?"

He nodded his head. She led him in the Sinner's Prayer. The next day when she went into his room an evident calm and peacefulness had settled on his face. His hands were folded on the white sheets of his freshly-made bed. She reached out and covered his hands with hers and asked gently, "Are you a child of God now?" He smiled and, without hesitation, replied, "Yes." He died the following day.

Esperanza nurses Beatrice Long, Shirley McLean, Dorothy Whiteside and Maise Wardale, 1948.

CHAPTER 12

Medical skills
and prayer
intertwined

The nurses in the early days were extremely dedicated to the McLean's and their work. Long hours were required for all who became part of the mission. It is reported that a tourist from the Maquinna, touring the hospital, was overheard saying, "I wonder who that nurse was? She could not be the matron because she was sweeping the floor," but of course it was. She not only swept the floors but also waxed and polished them. Along with patient care, the nurses kept the hospital warm by constantly stoking the wood stove. They kept the kerosene lamps in readiness by filling them, trimming wicks and polishing globes.

Medical cases were interesting in their variety: infection of the liver with amoebic bacillus, a heart case in extremus, and a case of hemorrhagic infarction of the lung with thrombosis. Dr. McLean also made a name for himself with the Workmen's Compensation Board for his skill in setting bones. It has been said that Vancouver General Hospital emergency staff knew that if a patient was sent to them from Dr. McLean, the patient's problem would not only be correctly diagnosed but everything would have been done for that patient that could have been done.

It was a hot sunny day in August when a fish boat tied up at the hospital dock and deposited George. "George from Privateer Mine," said the men who brought him in and then, they added, significantly, "Been on a drunk!"

Dr. McLean recalls, "If ever there was a hopeless looking wreck of humanity, George was just that! He was dissipated by weeks of drinking and worn out after a grim struggle for existence. Attack after attack of asthma had laid hold of him, threatening to snuff out that brittle thread which separated him from eternity—this was George when he first came to us. A 'wreck' indeed, debilitated physically and mentally but with 'soul-sickness' thrown in!

"I was about to commit suicide," he told us later. "In fact, I would probably have done so had I not been brought here, for I had just bought another bottle of whiskey to give me nerve enough to end it all."

George doesn't remember his first days in the hospital but, as kind hands cared for him and prayers ascended to the Throne on his behalf, the tired man relaxed and his worn body began to respond to treatment, until soon, he was well on his way to satisfactory recovery.

"The doctor used to come in and talk to me," George recalls. "I don't remember all that he said to me. I only know that I was sick of the old life and wanted something better. I pleaded with him to somehow keep me from going back to it."

As the claims of Christ were presented to him, George responded and received Jesus.

"While making my medical calls in a logging camp one evening," the doctor writes, "I found a young woman in dire distress. Five years earlier she had been entrapped by a drug peddler in

Vancouver and had become an addict. By that time she was taking from five to six grains of heroin daily, at a cost of $5.00 per grain.

"There are many such girls in our so-called 'Christian' land. Their only purpose in life has become to obtain enough money to buy this drug. So desperate do they become that they will do literally anything in order to procure their daily need. Many of them are sold, body and soul, into the white slave market. Addiction to alcohol is trivial in comparison.

"When I first saw her I did not know the cause of her trouble but I knew that she was very ill. I brought her to the hospital where she told me her story. In sheer desperation she had left Vancouver and travelled by airplane to the West Coast of the Island where she obtained work in one of the logging camps. Deprived of the drug, she had worked one day and then passed out. On the fourth day, I saw her and brought her to the hospital.

"The nurse gave her some medicine and we had prayer with her. She was suffering the agonies of hell: eyes bloodshot, cramps in bowels and muscles, headaches, watering eyes, stopped up nose. In fact, her symptoms were typical of one who had been deprived of drugs for some time. By the end of one week, in answer to her prayers and ours, she was taking only one-eighth of a grain of morphine in twenty-four hours. During the next week she had only three hypos and was trying to work.

"We had her in our home for a few days. She was not yet normal, but she did believe that God would deliver her; and, although she did not confess Jesus Christ as her personal Savior, we believe she is well on her way to recovery."

❧❀❧

The doctor writes, "It has always been our custom to have prayer in the operating room just before starting the anaesthetic. We were both surprised and pleased when a first-aid man from one of the camps told us that 'the boys' had quite often voiced their appreciation of our prayers on their behalf, and commented on the peace and security they felt in knowing the Lord was indeed present and was undertaking for them."

However, these prayers were not always interpreted that way. Some were frightened, thinking that the doctor prayed because he had neither skill nor confidence in himself. One patient who had to have an emergency surgery told a nurse afterward that he expected to die on the operating table. When she enquired, "Whatever put that into your mind?", the patient replied, "When I was going to the operating room, I saw in big letters on a board, 'Prepare to meet thy God.' I thought you were going to do away with me."

Medical skill and prayer were so intertwined that it is impossible to separate the two. The doctor writes, "To God be the glory, great things He has done! The prayer of faith shall save the sick and the Lord shall raise him up." (James 5:15.) "These signs shall follow them that believe, they shall lay hands on the sick and they shall recover." (Mark 16:18).

A ten-month-old baby was brought to the hospital one day and the doctor made the diagnosis of meningitis. The condition of the child seemed hopeless. Isolation orders were given and special medicines were administered. The baby cried unceasingly. That night was prayer night and one of the staff was asked to lead in prayer for the little one. In less than 15 minutes the child was asleep. The baby rallied miraculously and went home three days later in apparently perfect health.

A healthy young, man awakened one afternoon to find himself flooding with blood from his lungs. With much difficulty he made his way to the hospital in his own boat. He was immediately put into bed and emergency treatment administered. The staff prayed, asking God to assist. A few days later, he was much improved and said, "I give God credit for stopping the bleeding in answer to your prayers."

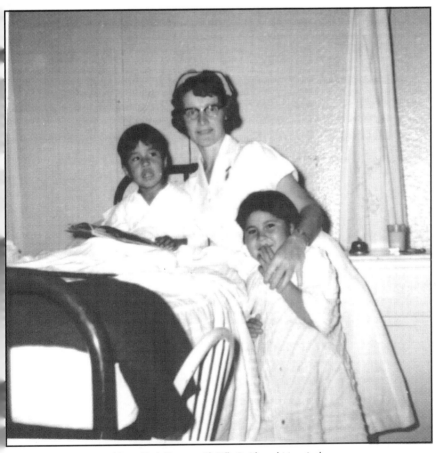

Nurse Ruth Kruger with Billy Smith and Mary Jack

Third Beach, near Camp Ferrier

Photo: Ross Scott

THE
NOOTKA
MISSION

Main Street, Zeballos, B.C., circa 1938

CHAPTER 13

Need for
the Good News
was everywhere

*L*ong before the hospital was ever established, there was considerable enterprise on the Coast. There were active canneries and fish reduction plants. There were Indian villages, gold mines and logging camps, but there was neither doctor nor hospital. There were no Protestant missionaries or chapels. There were Roman Catholic churches and priests on the reservations but no one at all to care for the spiritual needs of the other people. The area seemed an open door for both doctor and missionary.

Percy Wills followed the directives of his Toronto-based mission in that missionaries were expected to be totally itinerant. The mission owned no land; it established no churches; it settled in no specific spot. It's ministry was to preach the Gospel in all the isolated communities of Canada.

Percy travelled many miles with a pack on his back to logging camps, fishing villages, lighthouses and communities where there were new settlers. He travelled with Phillip Mack, a Ucluelet Indian, in a dugout cedar canoe over treacherous open waters to take the Gospel to isolated villages. He worked hard, with a dedication and earnestness that made the hardest of men stop and question him, saying, "You really mean what you preach, don't you, Percy?"

When Dr. McLean decided to build a hospital at Esperanza, he had every confidence that his work would be under the direction of the Shantymen's Christian Association, but it was not to be.

It was a sad day for Percy and the doctor when a letter came from the office in Toronto saying, "We are very sorry. To own land and build a hospital is an excellent idea but to have the hospital under our mission board is not possible. Our policy for our missionaries is to be totally itinerant. Dr. McLean will have to choose another mission board."

Percy said, "I'm sorry, Doc, you're on your own. I will do everything I can to help you, but it looks as if you will have to get your own board of directors."

On October 7, 1937, Percy Wills met with nine interested friends in Victoria and formed what they called "The Nootka Mission Association." It was called the Nootka Mission as the

Tahsis, circa 1940

mission was situated in one of the five sounds of the West Coast of Vancouver Island, Nootka Sound.

Percy Wills and Dr. McLean shouldered the entire responsibility of organizing and developing the mission and the hospital. It was a great sadness to the doctor when he realized that the difficult task before him was to be an isolated work without the support and help of an established mission. Even though Percy supported him and helped him in every way he possibly could, Dr. McLean felt betrayed by the Shantymen. The isolation and magnitude of the work compounded his impressions of being deserted.

Nevertheless, undaunted, Dr. McLean reached out into the communities for support. He required a board of directors for the hospital as well as a board for the mission. Before long he had both. They were loggers, fishermen and miners who wholeheartedly supported his endeavors and stood with him in the board level decisions. For thirty-five years men from these communities generously volunteered their time and wisdom in the important decision-making process involved in the operation of the Esperanza General Hospital as well as the Nootka Mission Association.

It was evident to Dr. McLean that most people were interested in a doctor, but not all were interested in a preacher. He had a deep inner compassion for the souls of people. He wanted to save people as much spiritually as he wanted to save them physically. Wherever he went, he expected arrangements to be made for him to have a service. Whether it be a cookhouse in a logging camp, or a school house in a village, or even a home, he made his intentions known. From many, he received resistance but, from others, acceptance.

The doctor's son Don often accompanied his father on trips to the camps or villages. He writes, "It was not easy for me to go with Dad. After we had made an arrangement to hold a service in a school or cookhouse, I would have to go door-to-door inviting people to come to the service. I took Shantymen papers with me and gave them to anyone who wanted to read them.

"Some of the men in the logging camps were rank atheists. They would try to tear me apart. They would curse to my face using the vilest of language and find great sport in insulting me." It was extremely traumatic for Don at first but he soon learned that if he was going to cower and be afraid, he would go away whipped. He decided he would continue accompanying his father whenever he could and go into the camps with boldness and cheerfulness.

"I decided that if anyone responded to me with a smart answer, I would respond with positive words and indicate to them that I knew what I was talking about. When I spoke to them eyeball-to-eyeball, they would respect me and the rebuffing would stop. They would listen, even though they may not agree." He adds, "They needed to hear the Gospel and they needed to believe it, too."

Dr. McLean was quick of mind and speech. Often the men in camps would seek to intimidate him. On one occasion a young man confronted him and said, "Well, Doctor, I hear you're quite a good horse doctor." Dr. McLean retorted without blinking an eye, "Yes, I have to be a good horse doctor to look after a bunch of donkeys like you."

Many were responding to the Gospel as a result of Percy and the doctor's zeal in preaching. During the 1940's, it was evident that churches needed to be built for those who wished to have regular Sunday services as well as Sunday school for their children.

Ceepeecee was the first community to construct a church. Several Indian people working in the cannery became converts and were grateful to have a church established for them.

When people in Tahsis suggested a church be built in their village, Gordon Gibson, the owner of the company at that time, graciously offered the mission a piece of land high on the hill. He also supplied the use of a bulldozer to prepare the land. Added to that, the company supplied all the needed lumber. Mr.

Norman, the head carpenter for the new mill volunteered his spare time to help build the church.

The church at Ceepeecee was also built on a knoll of a hill on the west side of the cannery. One night, at the close of the evening service, an ill-dressed man under the influence of liquor walked into the church. He did not sit down and wait for the service to close in proper fashion but, with a loud voice, he addressed the doctor, saying, "Doctor, I'm lost and I want to know the way of salvation."

Some of the young lads who were present nervously snickered at his intrusion. The man looked at them and said, "If you boys are going to make fun of me, I'm going. To be lost is a serious thing. I have been six years in the Army and Air Force. I have seen death and dying on every side. Before the war I studied for the priesthood. I studied for eight years. While I was studying, God spoke to me."

His eyes filled with tears and a serene hush filled the dimly lit room. He looked pleadingly into the doctor's eyes and said in a subdued tone, "Dr. McLean, I'm lost and I want to get right with God. Could I please talk with you alone?" The congregation was dismissed and, after a long talk and prayer, this man became another of the many who were finding the claims of Jesus Christ irresistible.

Dr. McLean was acutely aware of the medical and spiritual needs of the people in the Clayoquot area. There were numerous military men in Tofino and Ucluelet during the war, as well as loggers, fishermen and Indian people needing medical assistance. When young Dr. Andrew Karsguard came to Esperanza, to provide a much-needed holiday for Dr. McLean and his family, Dr. McLean spoke to him about opening a hospital in Tofino. Dr. Karsguard stopped at Tofino on his return trip and looked over the situation. There was a building already constructed for a community hospital but there was not yet a doctor chosen nor nurses appointed. Dr. Karsguard agreed to practise in Tofino.

Tofino Hospital, 1947 Dorothy & George Bennett,
Olga Bange, Hilda Richardson, Evelyn Wigmore
and Lavina Wedow

This hospital also became an extension of the Nootka Mission Association. It opened in September, 1944.

The first ten years of the Nootka Mission seemed to have been productive, as anyone on the outside looking in would deduce, but Percy and the doctor were acutely aware of the spiritual warfare directed at them. The doctor had prayed to go to "the toughest place on the West Coast." Their struggles did not ease as time progressed, but the two men were *not without hope.*

Percy expressed his awareness of the struggles in a letter to his prayer group in Victoria. The following is an excerpt:

July, 1947.

"How to write is my problem. I find forces closing in on us and I feel the tenseness of approaching warfare again. I have known it many times in my experience in the logging camps and the mining camps as well as amongst the districts of settlers but this seems different. It has the earmarks of opposition of powerful forces, which I should judge are religious and political. I do not fear them in the slightest but I respect them greatly and look to my armour to see that it is in the best shape possible.

"We cannot expect to enter the country of the enemy or engage his emissaries, without getting a blast or two. In past years, we have had everything but violence hurled at us in places. Newspaper outbursts, as well as arson have been two of the opposition's tactics. The enemy will probably trot out a couple of new ones here. But we cannot expect progress without it.

"No one seems to care one iota about what becomes of the Indian people. White men are exploiting them for their liquor interests. Young-sters from six to ten years of age are given cigarettes and taught to play poker and other card games. The need on the West Coast for the Gospel is staggering."

The results of liquor on the lives of both Indian and non-Indian people brought untold grief to the doctor. One night, a wedding party of six had come to the nearby hotel to celebrate. They drank all they could consume, then staggered down the dock to their little boat and headed out into a storm. As they were pulling away from the wharf, in the darkness, the SS *Princess Maquinna* was maneuvering toward the dock. They were unable to get out of the way and the Maquinna hit the little boat broadside. All six perished in the chilling water.

⁂

In 1945 the Nootka Mission acquired a lot in Tofino. A building purchased from the Ucluelet military seaplane base was trans-ported to Tofino to become the Wayside Chapel. This Chapel and the Ucluelet Evangelical Church of Ucluelet were a joint effort of the Nootka Mission and the Shantymen's Christian Association.

In 1948, the year of Bruce McLean's death, a powerful earth-quake hit Esperanza. The hospital building was so shaken that the three-story cement chimney was cracked from top to bottom.

In 1950 the cannery at Ceepeecee burned. Prior to that, the pilchards totally disappeared from the coast, wiping out the entire industry.

In 1950 a hospital was being built in Zeballos and Dr. McLean feared that the hospital at Esperanza would consequently be closed. His fears were unfounded.

Tofino Hospital fire, May 12, 1952

Photo: Dave Bond

The hospital building in Tofino burned in May, 1952. The village of Tofino formed its own board of governors and constructed a new building which opened in August, 1954.

Andy and Hilda Ritersgaard gave two lots in Ucluelet to the Nootka Mission Association in 1953. A building was purchased from the nearby Ucluelet military seaplane base and was moved onto these lots to become the Ucluelet Evangelical Church building. Today it is called Christ Community Church.

The years of hard work had taken their toll; in 1952, Dr. McLean suffered his first heart attack. He was weakened, but this did not alter his determination to serve the people of the West Coast, which he did until his death October 17, 1975. Mrs. McLean went to her final rest on October 25, 1987.

CHAPTER 14

Residential and local schools for native children

*A*s I (Louise Johnson) stood with a teenage friend in the chapel of the hospital her face was serious and pensive. A shadow seemed to cross over her eyes. Without looking at me or changing expression she said, "I always feel sad when I stand here." I asked why.

"When I was young I seemed to be sick a lot. My parents would bring me here for the doctor and nurses to look after. Many times I stood here by this window and cried as I watched my mom and dad leave in the boat. I was frightened to be left here by myself."

Glancing over to see if she still had my attention she hesitantly resumed talking in her characteristically quiet way. "All us kids had to leave home to go to school when we were six. I dreaded the day when the plane would come for us. We went to Christie Residential School on Meares Island across from Tofino. I did not mind the daytime when we were in school but, at night I would get so homesick for my mom I often cried myself to sleep."

By this time I had put my arm around her slender shoulder, realizing that she had many pent up emotions and needed to talk. We sat down on the couch nearby. She looked at me cautiously, debating whether it was safe to disclose more information. She looked away for a moment or two and then slowly and quietly proceeded.

"I always looked forward to coming home in the summer. It was so exciting to be with my family and aunties and uncles again. But there were so many of us kids, I always held back. I wanted to talk to my mom but I could not seem to find the chance. I wanted to tell her that I would rather stay at the reserve with her than go away to school. I wanted to tell her how lonely it is at school."

Carefully moving her long black hair from the front of her shoulder to the back, she looked at me keenly for the first time and said, "I think my mother would have understood but I was too shy to tell her."

Esperanza School, 1972

Although the local school board built a school at Esperanza in the mid 1940's, it was used for the children in the near vicinity. Along with the Esperanza children were those from Ceepeecee, Hecate and God's Pocket. Twenty children filled the one-room school to capacity.

The villages of Kyuquot, Friendly Cove and Ahousaht had elementary schools but Queen's Cove and Nuchatlahts were without schools. The children from these villages attended the Roman Catholic residential school at Christie near Tofino. At the age of six came the heart-wrenching separation of children from parents. It continued for four generations. The Roman Catholic children from other villages who wished to continue their high school education also enrolled at Christie. Some attended other residential schools in Kamloops and Mission City. The Protestant children travelled to the United Church residential school in Port Alberni.

There were several who graduated from the schools at Christie and Port Alberni. Some continued their education in trades or professions and did not return to the reservations. However, the majority of the young men and women did return. The schools had taught them to speak English but, sadly, had destroyed the children's knowledge and confidence in their own language and customs.

At the hospital, communication with the doctors and nurses was expected to be in English and, unfortunately, it was taken for granted. It was with great regret that missionaries realized, many years later, that they should have attempted to learn the native language as missionaries in other parts of the world had learned local languages. So much of culture and inner expression is encompassed in the language of any people.

Many Indian people appreciated the schools. One old man, who attended the Presbyterian school established in Ahousaht at the turn of the century, related, "The first meal of pork and beans

Dominic Taylor

I tasted, I was pleasantly surprised. I liked them so much I wanted to take some home for my mother to taste. Not knowing how to do that," he smiles, "I held my pocket open and spooned as much as I could into the pocket of my pants."

Carpentry, sewing and music were taught. These skills continue to be much appreciated. Several men from the schools at Christie and Ahousaht became good musicians. Two of the men, Dominic Taylor and Art Nicolaye, became the valued instrumentalists for the weekly dances at the cannery at Ceepeecee. Dominic played the piano while Art skillfully accompanied with his accordion. They could delightfully produce music full of the necessary swing and melody, causing shy people to rise from their seats and become involved in the light-footed dancing of the 1940's.

Dominic says, "Sometimes I would sit at the piano at the hospital and play some lively music." With his shy smile, he continues, "The doctor seemed to enjoy it. He would dance around for a minute or two. I liked to see him light-hearted once in a while."

⚜

Although education was necessary, and the schools did the best they knew how; and, although the schools were appreciated and many good experiences were enjoyed, there were sad changes occuring on the reservations.

As a result of the children's leaving home for school and returning only in the summer, a breakdown in the strong family ties and family teachings took place.

One mother told of her six-year-old coming home one summer and announcing, "I do not have to listen to you anymore. I listen only to my teacher."

Mothers longed to teach their daughters the distinctive art of West Coast basket weaving. Grandmothers wanted to teach the proper treatment of grass and cedar strips for the skillful weaving. Designs of whales and eagles and ravens and canoes had been carried down among families for centuries. Grandfathers longed to teach their grandsons family prayers, songs, dances, carving and the important customs of their people.

Helplessness and confusion devastated the people of the villages but did not completely destroy the faith and conviction that many had — that much of the Indian way of life was good, and that some, if not many, of the Indian teachings were good teachings. They began to find that many of the old Indian teachings were similar to those found in the Bible. With hope, the men began to teach at potlatches as was the old custom; and the younger women began to create beautiful beadwork and basket weaving again.

The schools, of course, cannot be faulted in their attempt to teach the children English and other helpfull skills for modern day living; but the way they went about it could have been much more caring and supportive of the Mother Tongue.

Unquestionably, the security and lifestyle of the past were being shaken.

❦

One young woman had come from Alert Bay to work in the cannery at Ceepeecee. She was unable to communicate in Nuu-chah-nulth, since she was Kwakiutl. She was very confused when she came to the West Coast. She had little opportunity for education and was heartbroken as a result of her home situation. "I was married the year I was sixteen," she says. "They were hard years when I had all my children, thirteen of them. I do not think I could have come through it all without Esperanza. Dr. McLean was a fatherly person. When I talked to him about my problems, he responded as if my problems were his own. Dr. and Mrs. McLean prayed with me. Some of the nurses prayed with me too. I felt that Esperanza people were my family. They seemed to be the only people who really cared about me."

Arthur Nicolaye at Aktis Island, 1945.
Carving a canoe for transporting supplies.

CHAPTER 15

A growing staff adjusts to boats and water

*P*ercy Wills wrote to his committee in Victoria, "Some time, I'm going to write a book, and the subject will be 'Bacon, Baloney and Bilgewater.'

"One peculiar thing about a boat is the smell that comes from the bilge. This smell is difficult to hide or disguise. It permeates everything. So, today, when I was cooking lunch for Skipper, I got out some noodles which some kind soul had put on board about two years ago. I put them on to boil. They smelled funny. I put some cheese in to cover up the smell. The noodles still put off that strong odor. Then I put some bacon grease and milk in. Still the smell persisted. I cut up some garlic sausage and put that in, thinking that was bound to kill the smell. By this time the galley was filled with a not-too-appetizing stink. When we sat down to eat the stuff, it tasted like bilge water. In fact, when we burped later in the day, we could still taste the bilge water."

In the summer of 1948, the mission had three boats: the *Messenger II*, the *Bedouin* and the *Elizabeth*. The *Messenger II* sank in October of that year. The other two boats had their share of difficulties.

Once, while the *Elizabeth* was being loaded with freight from the S.S. *Princess Maquinna*, she got her deck under the guard rail. This smashed her decking so badly it had to be removed. The *Bedouin* hit a large log in the fog and damaged her keel. After it was repaired she struck another log. Although the men had put it onto the ways and repaired her several times, she still seemed unsafe for use.

The *Elizabeth*, while under repair, had to be used as the school boat, picking up children at Ceepeecee, Hecate and God's Pocket. She had no cabin shelter for the driver and he had to operate her, exposed to the elements, in both fair weather and pouring rain.

In June 1949, the *Bruce McLean* was dedicated for the mission's use. This 24-foot, clinker-built boat, with its powerful inboard engine was a delight to Dr. McLean. Funds were donated by friends of the mission in memory of his son and the doctor appreciated the speed and efficiency of the vessel. This rugged craft served the mission for 30 years.

❧❀❧

There are five sounds carved into the outer coast of Vancouver Island. Nootka Sound is centrally located— between Barkley Sound and Clayoquot Sound on the south and Kyuquot and Quatsino on the north.

Esperanza was isolated, as were the other communities. Among West Coast people there is a strong dependency on one another—a lifestyle of hospitality and sharing. So, as much as the staff at Esperanza desired to serve the communities, there was also a need for the staff to recognize that, as individuals, they needed help too. They needed the fellowship and support of the people of the neighboring villages; in simple words, to learn the

boat or float plane, all potential staff members had to face the question of whether they could adjust to travelling by water. Could one cope with the uncertainties of the sudden storms as well as the knowledge that these waters are called "The Graveyard of the Pacific"?

Bob Sutherland, a prairie man, came to Esperanza one summer. There he met Shirley, Dr. McLean's eldest daughter. They married and a few years later felt they should return to Esperanza as staff.

Bob and Shirley (McLean) Sutherland's wedding.

"Shortly after we moved there," Bob recalls, "I had to take the small school boat to Tahsis. We got to the entrance of the Tahsis inlet and we were encompassed in the grip of a storm. I tried to turn around but the force of the wind was too strong. The wind was gusting so strongly I even had difficulty turning toward Tahsis. It took an hour to get to the dock there. It normally would take about ten minutes. In the midst of all this, I noticed that I was feeling very peaceful. Even at home that night the peace remained.

"Next day, I was out again. Another storm made up as we came to the open water heading toward Zeballos. We ended up spending the night with Mrs. Rustand at Haven's Cove (locally known as God's Pocket) about a mile from Esperanza. We could

assist Dr. McLean, was called for a medical visit to Zeballos. The water was rough, so I said, 'You cannot go alone. I will come operate the boat for you because the sea looks pretty bad.' We headed out and had quite a time getting there. On the way back, we were in one of the worst storms I have ever seen on the West Coast. Two big booms of logs had broken up at Little Zeballos. The windshield wiper broke. There were eight people on board that night. I thought to myself, this is it! We're going down for sure. We can never survive this storm.

"The rain, mixed with hail, was beating down on the roof of the cabin. The wind was relentless. It was dark and the spotlight started to flicker. I thought it might go out. The boat seemed to fall helplessly into the troughs of the waves. It was difficult to steer. It was a miracle that we finally arrived at Esperanza safely.

"When we awoke in the morning, logs were everywhere. The water looked as if someone had emptied a giant matchbox in front of the hospital. My thoughts flashed back to the night before. How could it be possible that I had seen only two logs? How could it be possible that we had not so much as grazed one as we pitched from wave to wave over the frenzied water?

"As I looked out the window, meditating on the miracle that obviously had taken place the night before, the verse came into my mind again: 'My grace is sufficient for thee, for my strength is made perfect in weakness'."

<hr/>

A weary nurse fell asleep while travelling from Nootka one afternoon. Some say Hilda Richardson's drowsiness may have been from fumes leaking from the motor. No one knows exactly what happened but she slipped unnoticed off the boat and into the icy water. Those at the wheel were concentrating on the water ahead, watching for debris and deadheads and were unaware that they had lost a passenger. Sometime later, they were startled at their discovery and turned back, scrutinizing the shoreline for any sign of her. Eventually they saw her standing on the beach. Being a strong swimmer, she had reached the shore without difficulty.

⚜

Men who had lived all their lives on the land, as Bob Sutherland had, were ill-prepared to meet the problems of the sea. The mission, always busy and always needing someone to operate a boat, seldom took into account the preparation required in order for a novice to learn boat handling and navigation.

One young man was on a run requiring travel through the dangerous entrance of Esperanza Inlet. It is a very narrow entrance and very rocky, indeed! Suddenly, the fog began to move in from the sea. He had never encountered fog before. Soon he was completely engulfed and could not see anything around him.

Unless a person is familiar with compass readings and charts, he is at a total loss in fog. The novice headed one way, then thought he was wrong so headed in another direction. He had never experienced such total loss of direction and confusion. He began to panic and eventually cried out to the Lord and said, "Oh, Lord, please let me see something." His spirit calmed somewhat and, in a few short minutes, he noticed the fog beginning to lift. Soon he saw the passage through the inlet and was able to proceed on his journey.

⚜

One night, a call came from a village. Someone was very ill and an Esperanza boat was needed to transport the patient to the hospital. Weather conditions were good so a young man, who had not had a lot of experience with boats, was sent to get the patient.

With the patient safely aboard he headed carefully toward the hospital but misread the buoy marking a sandbar and went on the wrong side. The vessel hit the sandbar and grounded. The falling tide compounded the matter and every effort to get off was to no avail. They sat there for several hours. Eventually, an oil tanker spotted them and took them directly to the hospital.

⚜

Then there was a time when three of the mission boats took the school children and their parents to Zeballos to present their Christmas program. When the program was over and they left the building, they were surprised to see a fierce storm in progress. After some discussion the decision was made to return home to Esperanza.

The fierce wind and blinding rain were interspersed with startling flashes of jagged lightning and unnerving crashes of thunder. Eventually, the three boats were docked securely and the performers were glad to remove their drenched clothing, crawl wearily into their nice comfortable beds to dream more pleasant dreams of Christmas.

⚜

The waterway is shared by all the boats that journey in the Sound. Most are friendly but, occasionally, there is the odd one that is not.

One night Dr. McLean was travelling back from Nootka on the *Bruce McLean*. He saw the light of a boat coming toward him and altered course to starboard. The boat turned toward him. The doctor then altered course to port. Still, the boat turned and came toward him. Finally, he stopped, put the Bruce in reverse and was backing up, trying to avoid a collision. The oncoming boat did not slow down but ran, at full speed, into the bow of the *Bruce*. The impact was so great that it sprung the planking and lifted the deck of the *Bruce*.

Aboard the offending boat were two young men who were

drunk. They had been thrown flat on their faces. The doctor got a line on their boat and pulled it alongside, securing it to the stern of the *Bruce*. He then struggled to get the men aboard and proceeded to the hospital where they needed some stitches for their injuries.

Several weeks after this incident, the doctor was issued a notice to appear in court. Apparently, one of the running lights on the *Bruce* had been out. Charges were laid against him and he was issued a fine.

⁂

Drunkenness, caused by the liquor consumption at the hotel next door, was a constant cause of worry and concern for the mission staff. Many lives were lost because of alcohol abuse. Prayers were made every day that people would be delivered from its power.

The hotel kept a lot of their liquor supply in a shed on the wharf. One night, some men stole some cases and packed them to the beach, putting them into the water below tide level. They covered their loot with rocks to prevent it from floating away. Later, in a drunken state, they took the hotel owner's boat and started off toward Zeballos.

The boat ran out of gas shortly after they left the dock. Finding a container of gas, they tried to pour it into the tank but they had neglected to turn the motor off and it was hot. Because of unsteady hands, the gas missed the opening and spilled all over. The fuel ignited and a raging fire ensued. One of the men jumped overboard and swam to the Esperanza airplane float. The other, grabbing a paddle, tried to paddle the burning boat ashore. There was much hollering and shouting.

Harold Peters, asleep aboard the *Messenger III*, was awakened by the commotion. He looked out the porthole and saw the flames of the burning boat. He quickly sprang into action, rescuing the man on the boat. Others of the community gathered to help extinguish the fire, and save the boat.

The men were taken to the hospital and given a warm bed for the night.

⚜

One night, in dense fog, seven men left the hotel by boat. They made their journey safely to the narrow bight which opened into the Tahsis Channel where they plowed into the rocks and split the bow wide open.

Instead of keeping the boat on the rocks and climbing out, they backed off and immediately sank in the deep, cold waters. All seven men drowned.

⚜

During the month of July 1960, the faithful old boat *Donna Dene* (actually christened *Dieu Donne—The Gift of God*) came to her final rest on the sands of Ferrier Beach. She broke her anchor line one day, in a storm, and was blown ashore and pounded to pieces.

A few days later, the clutch of another boat gave way; then, soon after, the entire engine broke down. Soon after that, the engine of the *Bruce McLean* went to pieces.

Purchasing and maintaining boats was a costly part of the mission's budget through the years. Daily, the boat operators faced unexpected hazards. No matter how careful and skillful they were, deadheads and floating logs were always a menace to safe boat travel.

CHAPTER 16

A rugged camp
for a
rugged people

A mother once asked, "What did you do at camp and what did you feed the children? My boys keep raving about camp."

Another said, "Do you ever give the campers a bath or a shower? My boys smelled so bad I could hardly get near them when they got off the boat."

Another, "I do not think my boy changed his socks for the whole ten days he was at camp."

However, these mothers all agreed that their children had had a wonderful time at Camp Ferrier.

※◎※

The name on nautical charts marking the location of the camp is spelled *Ferrer* Point. But somehow, over the years, the mispronunciation has become familiar and the camp is known as Ferrier Point Bible Camp.

By 1948, the mission was conducting three fairly large Sunday schools and two smaller ones every week. The teachers felt

Camp Ferrier 1948 – Don McLean, Director

something extra ought to be done for the children during the summer months. One day, the thought came to someone that a summer camp would be the answer. Their minds were directed toward the radar station that had been used during World War II.

The first camp was held in 1948. Bruce McLean was a helper that summer, since he was 14 years old by that time. Don McLean was the director. Assisting him were three students from Prairie Bible Institute — Victor Zacharius, Lloyd Stinson and Earl Johnson, who was later to become the superintendent of Nootka Mission. The camp was run for a period of ten days and thirty-two children attended.

❦

The buildings at Camp Ferrier had been left vacant since the war and seemed ideal for a summer camp. However, almost before the camp was over, it looked as if the expectations for future camps at the site were to be shattered.

Dr. McLean wrote, "Junk men bought the whole layout. They started to tear down the buildings almost before we got our things out of there. We felt pretty hopeless about it. I approached the buyer and asked him what price he would charge us if we purchased one large building. He quoted me the sum of $1,000. That was far too big an amount for us to pay, so I asked if he had an alternate offer.

He said, 'If you will take down six of the buildings, I will give you the other one." The doctor continues, "I did not know what to do. We had no men. We had no equipment. I did not know what to tell him.

"At the mission, we prayed because we felt so strongly that Ferrier Point was to be the location for the Bible camp.

"The answer came. The following summer five young students from Prairie Bible Institute came as summer workers. These young men tore down the five buildings and, at the same time, we were able to have another camp using the one large sturdy building that we chose to keep for ourselves."

By the third summer, 1951, word about the camp had reached the remote villages of the coast. Boys and girls came from Port Hardy, Coal Harbor, Kyuquot, Hot Springs Cove, Ahousaht, Tofino and Port Alberni.

Since there were no roads to the camp, all the campers had to be brought by boat through the treacherous open water.

Percy Wills, aboard the *Messenger III* relates, "The sea was very rough on that first trip. Many of the children were sitting in the

"Uchuck III" with Esperanza barge as supplies and leaders are maneuvered to Camp Ferrier beach with paddles and pike poles.

stern, seasick and throwing up continuously. I was fearful that someone might become so weak he might even fall overboard. "My imagination and helplessness got the better of me. I went down into the hot engine room, took hold of the railing around the engine and prayed. It turned out to be not as long a prayer as I expected. I did not know exactly what to pray. All I said was, 'Oh Lord, please give me your peace.' " And He did.

"As a child," writes Dorothea (Dottie) McLean, "I remember hearing the roaring ocean on the beach below and shivering with fear of travelling back home in it the next morning. I always stood at the door next to dad as we crossed the ocean. I was scared. 'Dad are we going to sink?' 'Yes, dear. Of course we're going to sink,' was always his answer. A bit confusing for a small child. He called me 'Skipper' because I always stood right next to him and used to drive the boat while he prepared his sermons."

Summer after summer, it was no small undertaking to get equipment and supplies across the open seas to Camp Ferrier . It is situated at Tongue Point, on Nootka Island , about 21 miles from Esperanza. Heading through the dangerous rocks from the Indian Reservation of Nuchatlahts and on through the unpredictable waves of the open ocean, the expansive circle of Louie Bay is a welcome sight, because at low tide, a one-mile stretch of beautiful, warm sand awaits. All equipment had to be barged to the beach, since the tide levels, as well as large breakers, made it unsuitable for building a float or wharf.

Dottie remembers: "When I was 12 years old, there were ten to twelve of us campers on the *Donna Dene* as well as two leaders. We were just around Nuchatlahts when one of the leaders yelled to me and Howard Plummer, 'you have been through here countless times. Come up on the bow and tell us how to get through these rocks and reefs.' We were shocked and a bit frightened but neither one of us said anything. I could not believe my ears that these Bible school students, who had come for summer work, were greenhorns and neither one knew where to go. I remember being shocked but we obeyed the command.

Howard and I laid out on the bow, heads hanging over the edge, watching for reefs.

"I gave directions as best I could but I was not sure—and still to this day would not know all the twists and turns and the exactness it needs. Every tide makes a different setting as well. All of a sudden, we saw shallow water—a reef!!

"We screamed in unison. Too late—bump! Scraping sounds were heard on the keel. We came to a dead stop—sitting in two feet of water. It was a sand bar. Now what? 'Are we going to sink?' I thought. The leaders gave orders to go ahead. Go to the left. Keep going. We had only begun the half-hour passing through the reefs. For the next while, I was glued to the water in front, panic feelings in my heart, certain I was seeing reefs every other moment. We made it to Ferrier safe and sound. I do not know how, but God — He looked after us. As dad would often say, 'God looks after drunks, missionaries and fools'."

One winter, a large barge was built for towing supplies to the camp. There was never a dull moment once a crew started preparing for camp. Mattresses were supplied by Joe Coleman of the C.P.R. stores in Victoria. A portable ramp was built to load a Jeep. The Jeep proved invaluable because it could be driven off the beached barge at the camp and then used to drive load after load of food, mattresses and other equipment up the hill to the buildings. Cabins were built as the number of campers increased. Lumber, nails and other materials were much more easily transported with the use of the jeep.

Each spring, there was much-needed maintenance for the weather-battered facility. The buildings were located on a hill where the wind and rain driven from the open ocean relentlessly deteriorated the wooden structures.

One winter's damage included an almost total demolition of the original large building. The kitchen and dining room occupied most of the space in the building. When the maintenance crew stepped ashore to open up the camp and begin their preparations for the campers, they gasped as they saw a huge cedar tree almost dividing the building in half. The tree had been blown down in the strong winds and lay precariously among the central beams. An extraordinary effort was required by the crew to meet the opening day of camp that year.

One year, a counselor wrote, "The mice seem to have totally taken over the camp. They are not a bit afraid of enjoying the camp with us." Another camp director organized a celebration for the entire camp on the occasion of the elimination of the one hundredth mouse!

When July approached, campers came by boat-loads. With everything in order and the camp in progress, one of the workers had the important job of keeping water on hand. The Royal Canadian Airforce station had put a pipeline across the beach, through a lagoon and up a mountainside to a spring—a distance of over a mile. Most of the pipe had either corroded in the salt water or was removed by the salvage company. A new source of water had to be found to supply the camp with fresh water.

Across the mouth of Louie Bay at a beach by the lagoon access, a source of fresh water was found. Using the raft and buckets and barrels, two of the young men assigned to the job conscientiously paddled across the rolling water every day. There they would fill the barrels with fresh water from the mountain stream and paddle the raft back to camp again.

Before the Jeep was available, a wheelbarrow was the means of conveying the precious liquid. The first delivery was made to the cooks. Two of the lads who had this task one summer, recall the freedom they felt as they paddled across the bay for the water. They would stand on the raft and sing to their hearts' content, as loudly as they wished, with nobody to criticize, challenge, or even hear them. The work was hard but it was always fun.

After 12 years of supplying water to the camp with raft and barrels, a waterline was installed. However, this had to be removed and stored every fall.

One of the staff, George Hardy, had found a large stove and a water tank in the foundation of the burned-out Esperanza Hotel (It burned in 1959.) These were ideal for the camp. Mr. Hardy and Orpan Hungerford donated enough funds to purchase water hose to reach the mile or so to the source of water the R.C.A.F. had used. The water ran across the beach from the mountain and lagoon into a tank on the hill. The system was fed, by gravity, from the mountain one mile away, to the hill by the camp and, thus, to the kitchen. Such luxury!

George Hardy inserted copper coils into the wood stove. Water from the tank circulating through the copper coils supplied the kitchen with lots of hot water. You can probably guess the first use of the hot water. George's wife, Karin, gathered some clean cloths and asked her husband to stand guard at the door of the kitchen. She filled the large smooth concrete sink and soaked her weary bones in the luxury of hot water.

George, with a hearty laugh, says, "I do not know, but I expect Karin is the only one who has ever had a bath at Ferrier. I put in a shower after that and most everyone has enjoyed a Ferrier shower, but not a bath."

⚜

Camp Ferrier is an extremely isolated place. There are absolutely no intrusions of sound from the commercial world, except for an occasional seaplane passing overhead. Only the wind, sometimes an owl, a chipmunk, or a sea gull interrupts the tranquility. The stillness is relaxing and gratifying.

Someone once said that, at Ferrier, even the silence is loud.

The daytime activities of hiking, swimming, competing in sports on the beach, playing volleyball and badminton, etc., generate huge appetites; and, after campfire, both campers and staff fall into their beds, exhausted. Snuggled in their sleeping bags, with their fellow campers closely packed on nearby bunks, each one feels a sense of safety, security and belonging. Sleep was deep.

Even though animals were nearby all the time, no one feared

to sleep on the beach around the campfire. Deer and mink were often nearby but focused on their own pursuits.

The personal, close contact of counselor and camper brought about friendships that, in some cases, remain meaningful to this day. As the truths of the Scriptures were shared for ten full days, many young people received help in answer to their prayers.

※

It was the custom of the camp for everyone to have a rest in their cabins after lunch. The fresh air and exertion in activities necessitated a rest time to restore the young people somewhat before the afternoon activities began.

During one of these rest times, a young camper had to leave the cabin to walk down a short incline to "Trinkle Inn", the outhouse. This particular one was near the garbage disposal. Junior campers never walk or saunter, they generally run. When he turned a corner in the trail, he faced a bear not five feet away.

The boy stopped in his tracks, turned and ran as fast as he could in the opposite direction. When he was about halfway back to the cabin, he realized that the bear was not chasing him, so he stopped. He quickly glanced over his shoulder and could see no sign of the bear. Slowly, he turned around. There was nobody nearby, since the others were resting in their cabins. So, he quietly started walking down the hill again, cautiously looking in every direction.

The bear was nowhere in sight. He stood quietly on the trail for a few minutes. Above him he heard a rustling in the branches of a tree. He looked up. The black bear was perched awkwardly only a few feet above him.

He rushed back to his cabin and told the counselor and campers he had met a bear out on the trail and it was in the tree. The siesta ended abruptly. The campers jumped out of their bunks and ran for the trail. As they got to the site, the bear was

Young voyageurs

Photos: Ross Scott

Camp Ferrier cave

Campfire days

slowly backing down the tree. The counselor thought it would be safer if the bear were up the tree, so he courageously chased it up again. By this time, the entire camp had heard the commotion and had come to experience another wilderness adventure.

✦✦✦✦✦

One summer, there were about fifty youngsters at the camp. With no refrigeration, frequent trips to Esperanza were necessary in order to obtain the necessary supplies of fresh fruits, vegetables and milk.

The boat operator, Joe McPherson, got up early one morning to make the trip in the *Donna Dene*. When he reached the beach, there was no boat in sight. It was a precarious anchorage and she had been sunk by a sudden storm in the night.

In those days, there was no radio communication. Joe hiked up the trail to the campsite and left word that, since the boat was at the bottom, he would have to row to Nuchatlitz and hitch a ride to Esperanza with some fishermen.

With four miles of rough water before him, Joe set out in the rowboat. When he arrived at the village, the fish boats were tied up. Some of the fishermen said in amazement, "Do not tell me you came from the camp in that little thing." He assured them he had and that his reason was quite important. The fishermen were having a "harbor day" (because the water was too rough for fishing); one of the boats took Joe and his skiff to Esperanza. Joe proceeded to gather the food and other necessities. Since no boat was available at Esperanza to take him back to camp, he moved the supplies down to the wharf and waited to hitch another ride by fish boat back to the camp.

Eventually, a fish boat came by and docked for the night. It was leaving for the fishing grounds at 3:00 a.m. and the skipper offered to take Joe and his load along. Since the camp is out of the way for fishermen who are heading for the fishing banks, Joe suggested he be dropped off at the Esperanza entrance buoy.

The skiff was lowered and tied to the buoy until all the supplies could be loaded. The waves were considerable, and Joe had to be careful for fear of swamping the skiff. The provisions were secured with a tarpaulin. The fisherman said "Goodbye," and Joe rowed the five miles back to camp.

✦✦✦

"I remember my last time as counsellor," relates Dottie McLean. "We left early one morning on board the *Bruce McLean* with approximately eleven campers heading home. Dad was the skipper. Sandy McLeod was first mate, so to speak. We had come across the open sea, through the reefs, just past Center Island, when suddenly the engine stopped. Dad and Sandy worked on getting it started. No way. Finally Dad said, 'Just a wee bit of gas in the carburetor.' The next thing I heard was an explosion!

"When I opened my eyes, the whole cabin inside was engulfed in flames. My first thought was to dash out the front passenger window . . . all the kids will follow . . . head for the reef . . . pull the skiff off and save as many as we could. I did so. All the kids followed. Then I noticed there were no flames coming through the roof. This surprised me, so I jumped on the side deck and looked in the window. There was Dad, snuffing out the fire with a sleeping bag. It was almost out. I said, 'What happened, Dad?' He said, 'I was engulfed with fire all around front and legs, but I had to put the fire out. God looked after me.'

"Now what? Fire was out. Cabin all charred and black inside. Sandy still hanging out the back trying to catch his breath. Kids all up on top, sitting, and scared.

"We floated for five minutes as such. The winds started whipping us toward shore. I could see more danger. So, I said, 'Dad, this skiff is light. I'm going for help.' 'Okay', he said, 'Be careful.'

"With my nose heading north, towards Steamer Point, I never stopped a stroke. It was seven miles. The winds were blowing two to three foot waves. But they were pushing me. I just made certain to sit on the crest of each wave and with everything in me rowed fast and hard. One hour later I steamed around the Hospital Point, heading for the Esperanza docks. Someone saw me. They waited at the dock. Caught the message, and flew to the gas docks to grab a fish boat to come to our rescue. They did. The Bruce was towed in. The kid's were happy to be back safe and sound."

With sparkling eyes and a far-off stare, a relaxed smile coming over her face, Dottie remembers, "I could write story after story with warm memories of Ferrier, as a camper and as a counsellor . . . ."

There are thousands more stories of others who were touched by Camp Ferrier; happy memories of simple joys among friendly and caring young people — treasures to last a lifetime.

Chrissie John with her daughters:
Agatha, standing; Alice "L", Dorothy "R", from the Ehattesaht band.

Photo: Dan McPherson

CHAPTER 17

Stories

of healing

O ne day both a mother and her daughter were admitted to the hospital for surgery. The little eight-year-old girl was fearful and tears streamed down her cheeks uncontrollably on the morning of her surgery. Although the nurses had tried to talk with her and comfort her, nothing seemed to ease her fear. Sobbing, she was carefully placed on the operating table.

The doctor and nurses held her little hands as they routinely bowed their heads praying for wisdom and guidance. After prayer, the circulating nurse asked her if she had learned any songs in Sunday school. She said, "yes" and promptly started singing "Jesus Loves Me". The doctor and nurses joined her in singing all the verses of the song. She then began to sing another song she had learned. Soon, her fear eased and she looked around to the doctor with a hint of a smile, indicating that she was ready. The anaesthetic was started and the little girl sang until her eyes closed in deep sleep.

When her surgery was completed and she was taken for post-operative care, the operating room was cleaned and the nurses prepared for the next patient — the little girl's mother. After the prayers were said, to the surprise of the staff, the mother also broke into song and she sang until the anesthetic took control, causing her to wander into sleep.

⚜

The tragic, as well as the delightful, constitute the life of any hospital. Many tragedies occurred. One spring morning the young lady, who was the first student in the Esperanza Bible School, awakened with severe chest pain. She was quickly rushed to the hospital. The doctors and nurses did everything they could to save her life. Her family was notified and many came to her bedside. As she lay dying, tears flooding her eyes, she pleaded with her brothers to stop drinking and let God be in their lives.

⚜

Heart-wrenching experiences are a part of the nursing profession but, at Esperanza, death affected many nurses perhaps more deeply than it might in a larger, more cosmopolitan hospital. Every patient coming for treatment seemed like a friend and a neighbor.

One nurse who had been enjoying her duties at Esperanza was shattered when a little Indian baby died in her arms. The doctor and the nurses had done everything possible to save the child, but to no avail. She had never seen a baby die before. "When he died, I felt so sorry for the mother. I was so overcome with grief that I went into the diet kitchen and cried. I was broken-hearted. I had grown to love him as if he were my own."

⚜

A young boy was admitted for a routine tonsil and adenoids removal. Dr. McLean had done the surgery, while Dr. Keith

Boughton had administered the anaesthetic. Dr. McLean was away the next day, when the nurse reported the patient was hemorrhaging. On examination, Dr. Boughton found the adenoid area bleeding steadily.

The adenoid area is impossible to see. They tried various methods of stopping the bleeding but every attempt failed. Sud-

Beulah Harnum, Director of Nursing, until Hospital closed in 1973

denly, the little fellow became violently ill and threw up a massive amount of the blood he had been swallowing. By then, Dr. Boughton saw that his patient was in serious shock, so they rushed him to the operating room and gave him an anaesthetic.

One of the nurses had recalled a new device that was on the shelf. It was very fine tubing containing a small balloon on the end. With the boy's head held back, the tube was inserted into one nostril and gently moved into his throat. When it was in the right position, the doctor inflated the balloon and pulled it firmly, anchoring the tube on the front of the little boy's nose. The pressure of the balloon on the adenoid area stopped the bleeding. The little boy recovered quickly and soon afterward returned home.

❦

In November, 1971, about 10:00 a.m., the sound of an airplane's engine, revving for the third time, alerted the maintenance man that a seriously-injured patient was aboard. Three or four people hurried to the dock in time to help the pilot dock the craft. They had to take time to tie the dock lines securely because a southeast squall was making up.

A logging camp had radioed to inform Dr. Boughton that one of their men had been hit on the head with a log and would be flown to the hospital as soon as possible. This information gave the doctor a little time to study his books and refresh his knowledge of head injuries.

The men and the pilot carefully carried the injured man up the ramp, along the sidewalk, and up the front steps to the main floor of the hospital where his condition was immediately assessed. The patient was in a three-quarters prone position on a stretcher, his head a mass of dirt and blood and he had lost consciousness. He would have to be flown to a larger hospital — one that was equipped to do brain surgery.

Leaving the care of the patient with the nurses, the doctor hurried to the radio phone and sought to have one of the airplane companies send a plane immediately. There was no plane available. Every plane was being used to transport people, mail and supplies. The doctor pleaded with the ground crew, saying, "Dump your load and please get here as fast as you can."

He relates, "I went back to the patient to assess his condition and it was obvious that he had deteriorated rapidly. It might be impossible for him to survive a plane trip, even to the nearest hospital in Campbell River."

A plane finally arrived. The patient's wife was aboard and she scrambled to the dock, rushed up the ramps and hurried along the path to the hospital. When she arrived, Dr. Boughton was shocked! He knew the woman and her husband and family. He had not recognized the man, due to his position and bloodied condition. This made the doctor's position even more personal and heart wrenching.

Further bad news arrived. Weather conditions were too bad to make a direct flight over the mountains to Campbell River. The patient would have to be flown to Gold River and then be driven by ambulance to Campbell River.

The patient would never survive the trip. If anything was to be done for the injured man, it had to be done now — and the doctor had to do it.

He informed the patient's distraught wife of her husband's critical condition, and that he was going to do surgery on his brain. Then, he added, "I don't know what is going to happen." He directed her to the home of one of the staff — a little cottage called "Seaside". Weakly, she knocked on the door and was ushered in to find herself in the midst of an intense prayer meeting. Many staff members had gathered to pray for her and her husband, and also to pray for wisdom and guidance for the doctor and nurses.

In order to move the patient to the operating room on the second floor, it was necessary to use a hand-operated elevator. This was operated by a chain and pulley system and, while it could carry heavy loads, it took several minutes to make the lift. This was too much precious time and the medical team decided to convey the patient out the front door and up the outside fire escape stairs to the operating room.

Four nurses and the doctor quickly set to work preparing the operating room and the patient. Not one had been involved in anything like this before at Esperanza. Supernatural peace descended on the team as they worked together—a brave crew, sailing in uncharted waters, rising to meet unknown challenges — this was the essence of Esperanza!

There was no facility for a blood bank at Esperanza. When blood was needed, it was flown in from Vancouver. The medical staff realized that an emergency might arise where a patient's life might be saved if the staff were prepared to donate blood. All the staff had been typed and cross-matched. One of the nurses had been assigned the job of getting the precious pints of blood.

A number of staff lingered near the operating room while she set up the intravenous tubing for her first experience at taking blood from donors. The urgency of the hour motivated her to such an extent that she felt completely competent to gather blood from the "O"-type personnel. Inserting the needle into an available vein of the patient, she started intravenous blood drip, without once asking questions or troubling the surgery team as they concentrated on the emergency at hand.

One of the patient's pupils was dilated and fixed. His respirations were literally disappearing and becoming slower and slower. His pulse was weakening, indicating the slowing down of the heart. At this point he had no spontaneous movement in any of his limbs. Prayers were being uttered as everyone concentrated on the surgery. Peace and order attended the competent team, dispelling any tendency to nervousness as they diligently performed their duties.

With the scrub nurse standing equipped to help on the opposite side of the operating room table, the doctor, using a scalpel, cut a large skin flap above and behind the ear, exposing the skull bone. A special burr hole drill for the skull was not on hand. The only available instrument was a screw-type drill designed for putting screws into broken leg bones. The other substitute instrument was one used for trimming bone.

Since there were some cracks in the skull, the young doctor was able to dig the trimming instrument under the edge of the crack and nip pieces of bone. In this way, he was able to enlarge the hole enough to diagnose the problem. It was evident that there was a blood vessel which was torn and bleeding. Inside the skull was a massive blood clot, about an inch thick all over the entire half of the brain. This was creating tremendous pressure on the base of the brain—a condition called "coning"— where the heart and lungs are in danger of ceasing to function.

They had to work quickly now to make their way through the clot and find the tear in the artery. The clotted blood was thickening to the consistency of jelly. It was too thick to suction out, and proper instruments were not available. A nurse was sent to the kitchen for a spoon. This was sterilized, and used to scoop out the "jelly". Eventually they were able to locate the bleeding artery and the doctor sutured it, thus stopping the bleeding.

By this time darkness had crept over the water and the stillness of evening had settled on the grounds. The scrub nurse stood up and, moving her shoulders to relieve the tension, spontaneously said, "Praise the Lord." Smiles broke out and everyone knew that, now, their patient had a chance to live.

"If the bleeder had been inside the dura, it would have been unquestionably fatal in anyone's hands. He is a very lucky man," the doctor said, breathing deeply with relief, the crisis over.

They settled back to work again. It took some time to evacuate the clot. During this process the patient began to regain consciousness. Pain medication had to be given to settle him. The large skin flap was sutured. There was nothing that could be done about the skull piece that had been laboriously cut out with makeshift tools. The patient's vital signs steadily improved as the nurses vigilantly attended him for the next 24 hours.

Next day his condition was stable enough for him to be flown to the Vancouver General Hospital. The surgeon in Vancouver was surprised by the accomplishments of the team. No further treatment was necessary until it was time to put in a bone replacement flap.

The patient was back at work in six months.

Reflecting on the incident, Dr. Boughton says, "If that logger had been the only person I had worked on during my five years at Esperanza, it would have made my time worthwhile there. The textbook and a lot of prayer were the basic essentials for the whole process. With it, I had a driving determination that this was something that had to be done well, and it had to be done thoroughly, and it had to be done now."

⚜

In the village of Kyuquot, about forty miles north of Esperanza, Jackie Whan was the nurse in charge of the Red Cross Outpost Hospital. She and Lorna Penner had both been nurses at the Esperanza General Hospital before it closed. They moved to

Kyuquot in the early 1970's and conscientiously cared for the physical and spiritual needs of the people.

One December morning an expectant mother started labor pre- maturely. The weather was too inclement for planes to fly that day. Another registered nurse was visiting at the time, so they prayed that the delivery would be normal.

The nurses prepared all their equipment for the delivery and warmed the little crib for the baby. The delivery was without any complications but the baby was reluctant to breathe. The young mother was frantic, as the nurses worked on the tiny person. Occasionally, the baby would show signs of gasping for breath. There was no modern equipment to work with.

The young mother was grieving over her own mother's death and the nurses knew that God would not be unkind and allow this baby to die. They worked with determination and unusual faith.

For an hour and a half they resuscitated the tiny body. They were persistent and gentle and careful. The little limp body stretched, then squeaked, then began to cry in a loud compelling voice — sweet music to their ears. Her brown skin flushed with life; she was alive. The nurse holding her cuddled the little form close to her breast as tears of joy erupted from her eyes. The mother wept uncontrollably as she was given her baby to hold and to snuggle and to express her joy and thanks to God for giving life to her little girl.

The nurses did not sleep as a storm lashed the small two-story hospital. Throughout the night they vigilantly cared for the mother and the child as the wind whistled around them.

As soon as the marine radio office opened in the morning, the airlines were called. A pilot from Tahsis courageously set out for Kyuquot in a Beaver, with a stretcher wedged between the seats. The storm had eased somewhat, making the landing of the seaplane possible. He planned to return to the hospital in Tahsis. However, this was now out of the question. He could see that the storm was ravaging the Esperanza and Tahsis inlets, making a landing impossible.

He made the decision to fly the 90 miles south to the Tofino Hospital—on a wing and a prayer—so to speak. Jackie, the nurse, had written in detail for the doctor, information about the delivery and the time it took to revive the baby. Immediately, the doctor in Tofino contacted a specialist in Vancouver. When the weather improved, the baby was flown to the Vancouver General Hospital for assessment.

The report came back to the nurses in Kyuquot that the little baby girl was perfectly normal. There seemed to be no evident neurological problems whatsoever. The little girl is eleven years old now and the doctor in Vancouver was correct. She has absolutely no affects from her difficult first hours. She is normal. She is an answer to prayer. She is Pricilla.

Back row: Kathy Carter, Virginia Jack, Jessie Smith, Colleen John, Chrissie John, Arnold John.
Middle row: Earl Johnson, Beatrice Sam, Suzanne Karllson, Alice John, Lorraine John,
Louise Karllson. Front row: Louise Johnson, Michelle Sam, Rose Anne Billy, Angie Billy,
Karen Smith, Jennifer John, Dorothy John, Ruth Steer.
Seated at front: Michael Oscar, John Karllson.

CHAPTER 18

A *new era*

of

service

*A*mong those to meet us (Earl, the children and me) at the dock that day in March, 1972, were Dr. Keith and Nancy Boughton, Dave and Marlene Scott, Elvin and Helena McMann, Dave and Alice Breithaupt, Miss Fanny Carlile, Miss Lillian Parry and Mrs. Margaret Manning.

The days ahead were busy. Everyone was making last-minute preparations for the Annual Spring Conference and the official meeting where Dr. McLean would turn over the leadership of the mission to Earl.

Guests came by boat and seaplane. Many arrived on the *Uchuck III* late at night. Both staff and guests greeted the new arrivals with festive and sometimes tearful joy as old friends were reunited, young children were introduced to old acquaintances, and "the good old days" at Esperanza were remembered. Later, the singing of well-loved songs in four-part harmony brought tears to the eyes of many who fondly remembered learning those songs there, so long ago.

Saturday afternoon all the formalities were performed. Dr. McLean solemnly released the responsibility of the mission to

Earl, who appropriately accepted the position as superintendent of Nootka Mission. That night Dr. McLean delivered his last message to his Esperanza staff and the many guests who gathered in the gymnasium. The text of his speech included the following: "I sent a letter to the Succession Committee and gave them one hundred per cent responsibility for choosing someone to take my place. The Committee unanimously voted to ask Earl if he would come."

Louise and Earl Johnson, 1980

A fundamental principal of the Mission was to respond to the needs of the community; and, as a living organism of society, the Mission, in responding to those needs, was always in a state of transition.

In 1972 the Board of Directors decided to close down the hospital. Their reasons were obvious. The population of Tahsis was growing (approximately 2,000 by then), and logging roads to Tahsis and Zeballos had been made into public roads and were considerably improved and well maintained. Too, the provincial health insurance department felt that any funding for hospital expansion and improvement would be better employed at Tahsis.

The anticipated loss of hospital revenues would result in a considerable impact on the Mission and its staff, and its role of service to the community had to be re-assessed.

One serious concern was the lack of adequate dental services in the area. Dr. Robert E. Patton, of Vancouver, B.C., dentist, and member of the board of directors at the time, was instrumental in recruiting colleagues to establish a modern facility for treatment and education.

In addition to serving the dental needs of the community, this program helped generate revenue which allowed the Mission to carry out its other important work — ministering to the spiritual needs of the community, continuing the youth program at Camp Ferrier, helping (and sometimes shielding) those who were experiencing intractable family difficulties, and helping with alcohol-related family stresses and alcohol abuse.

Later, the Mission, working with the provincial Ministry of Human Resources, churches, and the courts, accommodated individuals and families for varying time periods, helping them to get back onto the road to recovery.

Again, it was a case of responding to the needs of the area. Leaders from the Nuchatlahts and Ehattesaht bands approached the Mission to co-operate with School District No. 84 in establishing a school for their children. A school was established in co-operation with the Ministry of Education and the Department of Indian Affairs. The necessary funding was received to equip and operate the school, hire an accredited teacher, and operate a school boat service. The Ministry curriculum was followed.

In the late 1970's, negotiations were opened with the Esso oil company and the provincial government for the upgrading of the fuel dock and service center. The docks were extensively rebuilt and new fuel tanks were situated in a concrete "tank farm". The facility was much appreciated, and well patronized by boat operators using the Inlet.

A large power plant building was constructed, complete with an efficient, new diesel generating engine.

The boatways and workshop were expanded and improved. A new roof was added to the boatways. Wings were also added to provide for carpentry and machinery work areas and respective supplies.

The *Lady Carlile*

Later, a 24-foot speedboat, the *Love Joy*, was donated to the Mission, by a supporting church in Seattle.

The 34-foot *Patsy* (a gillnetter) was given to the Mission by Joe Smith of Queen's Cove. Required alterations were made by shipwright Bruce Good and the vessel, renamed *Lady Carlile* (after Fanny Carlile), was launched in 1985, a testimony to Bruce's excellent craftsmanship. Many churches and

Bruce Good

individuals generously contributed finances, equipment and their time to ensure that the vessel would be safe and shipshape.

During this time, it is a credit to the staff who had the responsibility for insuring a steady inflow of funds in order to keep the Mission work going, and progressing, during difficult times.

Further, it is a credit to the work parties who helped in the maintenance and repair of the facilities; hundreds of friends,

Joe Smith

too numerous to mention here. Without their generous contribution of time and personal expense, the Mission could not have continued.

Throughout this period significant relationships developed with numerous support groups. Various church groups, from Bellingham and Seattle, WA, and Vancouver, B.C., not only significantly improved the facilities and generously provided equipment but also provided a major part of the financial requirements of the Mission.

Also, many staff members contributed significantly to the growth of the Mission. They came with diverse backgrounds, and applied their knowledge and skills in a multitude of ways. Sometimes their preconceived ideas about mission work on the West Coast were in conflict with the reality of the hour.

Jack Hill writes, "When I went to Esperanza, working in maintenance was exactly what I wanted. I didn't realize that God understood technical things. I was aware that He knew everything but it had never entered my head that I could be in a place of ministry using the talents the Lord had given me, using my hands, not my voice.

"It wasn't very long after that I was working on the boat called *Sea Splendour.* It was in the dry dock. We had installed new engines. They had run a bit but not much yet. I was lying on top of one of the engines trying to get the spark plugs out of the back side. I was almost upside down and I was getting really frustrated. I was frustrated that I couldn't get at the engines properly. I wasn't frustrated in what I was doing but just annoyed that the engine was so hard to get at. Of course, this is a typical problem with most boats.

"In that awkward position the Lord spoke to me very clearly and brought to my mind a question, 'Do you remember what you said to Me a few years ago?' The question was so clear to my spirit that I straightened from the clumsy position and stood between the two engines and answered in an impatient voice, saying, 'No! What?'

"He brought to my mind those words I had spoken to Him years ago, when I was still a teenager. 'If you had some hot engines to work on, I'd consider serving you full-time.' Here I was, eight years later, serving God full-time on hot engines. I mean they were the hottest marine engines Chrysler made that size. They were a guy's dream, that is, a dream for one who works on engines and understands designs and that sort of thing.

"Then the Lord said one more thing to me, 'Is this hot enough for you?' I burst out laughing. . . ."

Dan McPherson tells it the way he saw it. He wrote in his diary, "My job description: maintenance of diesel generator, grounds keeper, ramp builder, plumber, lawn mower, lawn mower repairman, fuel pump repairman, garbage man, incinerator cleaner, rat exterminator, Suburban [station wagon] repairman, chicken house builder, electrical linesman, school boat operator, goods handler (transporting groceries to people's houses), fuel oil delivery man, assistant chicken farmer and light bulb replacer."

Neil Harmsworth reminisces, "My first impression before coming to know the Lord was that the Mission was some kind of weird cult. Cults were big news back then with the Jimmy Jones affair shocking the world. Not knowing what it was, I had decided Esperanza was some kind of a nutty cult and figured that everyone must be on drugs. They were all smiling so much they had to be. My first impression after I became a Christian was that it was a great place."

Neil continues, "Everyone who comes here goes through a honeymoon period. Everything is bliss and wonderful. Afterwards one gets into the lessons and education of character and things get a little tougher."

In the natural course of events there are the inevitable misfortunes. It was a sad day when the *Bruce McLean* was lost in a prolonged sou'easter at Camp Ferrier. She seemed a tireless workhorse and had served the Mission faithfully for over thirty years. There was also a fire in the dormitory which resulted in a total loss.

During these years, Earl Johnson had the good fortune to have had the support of many capable and talented staff leaders. They made an outstanding contribution to the Mission in terms of program development, and in the vital work of helping their staff to grow and experience the joys of mission work. Many people, both young and old, worked under the capable direction of Elvin and Helena McMann, Ken and Sandy Brook, Jack and Myrna Hill, Mike and Rhea Ready, Dave and Marlene Scott, Rolf and Vivian Burnie, Dan and Isabel McPherson, Neil and Kathy Harmsworth, and many others.

1976 – Ken and Sandra Brook and son Peter. Presently serving in Zeballos.

During the 1980's the Board began to think about the similarity of programs that were being carried out by both the Nootka Mission and the Shantymen's Christian Association. In many ways, the policies, the purpose, the philosophy and outlook were similar to those of the Shantymen's.

In the early days it was the Shantyman, Percy Wills, who saw the desperate need for a hospital in this area. It was Percy who encouraged Dr. McLean to establish the Mission. It was Percy who nurtured the Doctor and his staff in the difficult early years as the Mission had to established its own Board and develop a support system.

Over time, organizations and their policies change to meet the changing times, and while the Shantymen policies and objectives were, by this time, basically unchanged — i.e. taking the Gospel to the far-flung communities and isolated people of Canada — one significant change was in regard to the ownership of property. In any region, if it is in the best interests of their mission work, it is now permitted.

It should be further noted, that most people in the area thought that the Shantymen organization operated the hospital, since Percy had played such a major role in the beginning. This ownership misconception by the people was further reinforced when Earl Johnson became the superintendent of the Mission. (Most people on the coast had first met Earl as a Shantyman, and still regarded him in this role.)

In 1989, discussions relating to merger began between the Nootka Mission, led by Board Chairman, Dr. Bob T. Patton, business consultant of Bellingham, WA, and the Shantymen's Christian Association. An agreement was reached and the Shantymen's organization assumed responsibility for the work at Esperanza on January 1, 1989.

The transition was an easy one. The responsibility for the Mission (now known as Nootka Mission, A Ministry of Shantymen International) comes under the direction of George Rieger, Field Director for the Pacific Region. Earl now serves under the Shantymen's Christian Association as minister at large for Vancouver Island. The work continues. Most noteworthy of all, the purpose, philosophy and outlook of the Mission continues as always.

Dr. McLean would be pleased.

Earl Johnson, Paul Smith and Rick Lindholm, 1979

CHAPTER 19

Dentists
expand their
services

*A*fter the hospital closed in 1973, the staff at Esperanza assumed that the dentists would also withdraw their work in the area. The assumption was wrong. The Christian dentists, directed by Dr. Robert E. Patton, expressed their desire not only to continue the dentistry they were already doing but also to expand the clinic and make even more services available.

Also working to establish the new clinic were Dr. Gary Hall, Dr. Vic Pauls, Dr. Ed Penner, Dr. Irwin Leitz, Dr. Dan Cheng, Dr. Bill Foreman, Dr. Grant Rawstron, Dr. Bruce Kennedy, and Dr. Egon Nikolai.

It would be a gross understatement to say that a new facility was needed. Many years ago the basement room of the hospital had been prepared as a makeshift arrangement. An old vacuum cleaner had been made into a fairly effective suction unit. Two dental chairs had been installed. One was an antique, complete with drill and, if nothing else, it served to stimulate the sense of humor of all the dentists who arrived.

Added to this, was the other deteriorating equipment. The main dental chair had a round, white marble tray for the dental instruments. This tray moved on an elbow that could be placed conveniently for the dentist.

On one occasion, from some unexpected source, a water leak sprang near that elbow. The dentist improvised a solution by wiring a tin can to the tray which accumulated the drips. Things had been going fairly smoothly and the leak had been forgotten, until the patient was getting out of the chair. In the process, he knocked the almost-full can of water into his lap. In the midst of the embarrassment, the dentist eased the awkward situation by saying, "Well, this is the first time in my practice of dentistry I've ever had a patient kick the bucket."

This uplifting, easy manner characterized all the men. The Esperanza women, assigned to assist, were untrained. The assisting techniques, the use of instruments, the X-ray procedures were patiently taught to each by the dentists. Dedicated to a high standard of dentistry, the dentists cared about the enormous dental needs of the people of Nootka Sound.

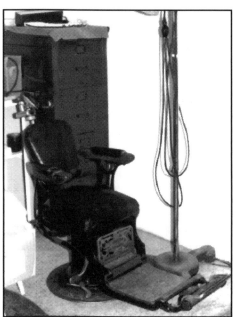

Antique Chair - early days of Esperanza Clinic.

Many people in the area had never had an opportunity to have proper dental care. They had never had the opportunity to learn about preventive dentistry. Many believed that dental treatment consisted of extractions and dentures as the only solutions to their problems.

The dentists saw the need to upgrade the quality of dental services to the community. They started organizing the existing supplies at Esperanza. They began to improve the facilities and upgrade the equipment. They chose the sunny location of the former children's ward and the private room across the hall. Proper plumbing, wiring and lighting were installed.

The British Columbia Department of Health provided dental care in most out-lying communities of the province, however, the trailers equipped for this service could not withstand the rough routine journeys over the logging roads in the Nootka area. As a result many communities were not provided with service. The volunteer dentists at Esperanza felt that the Mission alone could not match the level of dental care which was being provided in the rest of the province, and that the Department of Health should be invited to assist with the funding.

Dr. Patton invited some Department officials to assess the needs of the community and determine the level of support which the Department felt would be adequate. A study was undertaken, and the result was that the Department agreed to support the program. Funding was provided to purchase modern equipment and upgrade the facilities, and this resulted in a first-class treatment center. Now the dentists could provide a high standard of dental care — equal to any other treatment centre in the province.

The dentists often worked until midnight on dentistry weekends, returning exhausted to their homes in Vancouver. On one occasion, Dr. Dan Cheng, along with an untrained assistant, saw patients from 8:00 a.m. until 6:00 p.m. They were both exhausted by supper time. There were so many patients, initially, that most had only an X-ray taken and, maybe, a filling. The meal was pleasant and, to sit down and rest weary feet and legs was welcomed.

Outside, the sound of a seaplane slowing its motors was heard. Then another could be heard as its roaring engines eased for a landing. The dentist and his assistant both put their heads in their hands for a moment, and one said, "I hope it isn't more patients."

But it was. Work went on until midnight. The dentist said

later, "I enjoyed the work in the evening most of all." Was it that he enjoyed the people from Kyuquot most of all? Or had the Lord given him a special strength? Or was it both?

The dentists taught the helpers how to organize appointments. They taught charting techniques. They taught tray arrangements and the use of instruments. They taught the operation of the X-ray equipment. Bit by bit, those assigned to the dental clinic became more competent helpers. Although the workload remained heavy for the most part, more was being accomplished and the night hours were eliminated. Vivian Vasby, Myrna Hill, Sandy Brook, Eleanor Snyder, Joan Edward, Sharon Johnson and myself were among those who were trained in the dentistry program.

More dentists came to the Esperanza dental clinic. Students from U.B.C. came with their beloved professor, Dr. Ted Hyde. Dr. Gary Kirstiuk came from far away Williams Lake.

Occasionally, a volunteer was not informed about the water landing of the Mallard airplane at Tahsis. More than one had the sudden fear that their end had come and that the plane was on its way to the bottom of the ocean. Added to the adventure of the flight, was the boat trip from Tahsis to Esperanza. The mission's small outboard boats were a new experience for many and the voyage was often rough. When they arrived, they were generally hungry and sometimes travel-weary. The hunger could be remedied but weariness was ignored because patients were already waiting for their scheduled appointments.

The patients, too, had to come to the clinic by boat or seaplane. If the weekend progressed as planned, all went well. But often the best of plans can go awry. Sometimes a storm made up, making it impossible for a boat load or plane load of patients to come. Sometimes a weekend was over-booked and some patients had to return home without the necessary amount of treatment that was hoped for. For the most part, however, the weekends were a pleasant and satisfying experience for all. For the dentists, an occasional fishing or hunting trip was arranged or a trip to Ferrier Point added to the sharing in the overall experience.

Many people expressed their fear of having dental work done. One man was brought in by some friends from a bunk house in Tahsis. To ease his toothache, he had been drinking whisky all night. His buddies, hearing about the clinic, carried him in and set him in a chair. The dentist examined his mouth and took an X-ray while the drunken patient was totally oblivious to what was happening to him. After the offending tooth was extracted, his friends carried him back to the boat and returned to Tahsis. The fearless patient had no recollection of the experience.

Dr. Gary Hall, dentist with assistant. Dr. Hall was a founding dentist at The Dental Clinic

Another lady came prepared for imagined torture of some kind. She was pacing around the waiting room. The receptionist asked her if something was wrong. She said, "Oh, I'm so nervous, will you please tell me when I should take some valium?" She was assured that the dentists who came to this clinic were gentle and very kind and that she did not need valium. When her work was finished, she smiled and said, "You were right. I had no idea that a dentist could be so gentle."

The dentists were often saddened by the needs of the people. Some mouths were so wasted by tooth decay it posed a challenge in establishing a program of restoration. Should a number of teeth be pulled on a 16 year-old patient or would it be wise to do a root canal? Would a dentist return in sufficient time to continue in the second step of the program? Many three- and four-year-old children had extensive tooth decay. Some had only fragments of baby teeth. Dental hygienists were later brought in and teaching began. Children would come asking for the red disclosing tablets which, when chewed, would leave red stain on the areas of teeth being improperly brushed. Drinking juice or milk, rather than pop, was recommended. Proper brushing and use of dental floss was encouraged. Families took pride in their six-month check-ups once their children had no further decay. Fluoride treatment was given and the results were evident as the years progressed. The communities in the entire area became aware of their dental responsibilities. The obvious happened — dental needs diminished.

Many of the Christian dentists wanted to be active in reaching the people with the Gospel, but the dental work was so time-consuming that there was little time left to share in Bible teaching or visiting.

However, on one occasion, Dr. Vic Pauls and his wife, Joan, were working with the Vancouver-based evangelist, Terry Winter. They had offered to stay some Sunday and share their love for the Lord Jesus with as many people as could be rounded up. Of course, they had dental patients in mind. The ladies of the mission decided to have a salmon barbecue before the service. The men of the staff asked, "Where are you going to get the salmon?"

The answer was, "Well, you're going to catch the fish." Surprisingly, they did. There were over a hundred people who attended. A chef from the Tahsis Chalet came to preside over the occasion. The lawn by the Esperanza Coffee Shop was attractively set up for the feast. The outside barbecue emitted a scrumptious aroma as the marinated fish sizzled and fried over the open coals. It was a delicious feast. There was lots for everyone. Over the years, most people have asked if salmon can be caught off the dock. The answer we give is, "Well, we 'caught' lots from there the time we had the barbecue for our dental patients." (It has also been confessed, by a few men, that it is sometimes possible to "catch" fish right off the end of the dock — with a little help from the passing fish boats.)

After the feast, we gathered inside for a service led by Dr. and Mrs. Pauls. With humility, they shared their own lives. They told the group gathered that they did not have all the answers to a perfect life, neither had they lived perfect lives. They told of situations with which many of us could identify.

It was a special day—one man and his wife sharing their life with the community and responding to its needs.

How did the ministry of dentistry help the children? Obviously, they would appreciate, especially in their later years, the training they received in dental hygiene and care of their teeth. This one story of gratitude will typify the impact the amiable dentists had on many of the young folk.

A little girl came to the clinic with a neighbor. Her mother was

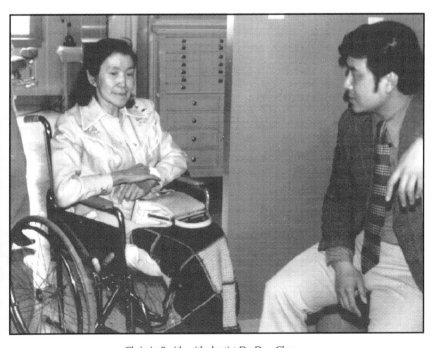

Chrissie Smith with dentist Dr. Dan Cheng

extremely frightened of the water. (Probably she would say she was terrified to travel on small boats—and some frightful experiences had given her good reason.) When her daughter needed to have her teeth examined, there was no way she could muster the courage to come to Esperanza on one of the mission boats. Her neighbor, knowing her fear, offered to bring the child. The little girl was nervous and anxious about the trauma she expected in the dental chair.

The dentist, responding to her apprehension, took time to play with her and explain what he would be doing. He gained her confidence and proceeded with her complete co-operation. When the remainder of the patients had been cared for and the boat was ready to leave for Tahsis, the little girl seemed a bit hesitant to go. When she stood on her tip-toes trying to see over the desk, the receptionist asked what she wanted. She said, "Can I see the dentist?" He put down his instruments and came over to the desk. She looked at him timidly and reached out her little hand to him. He smiled broadly and responded by kneeling beside her and putting his hand out toward hers. Into his hand, she placed a ten-cent piece; and, looking intently into his eyes, she said in her tiny voice, "Thank you for my tooth."

During their time at Esperanza the dentists probably had no idea that their kindness, their love and their very presence ministered to many of the hurting, lonely people in a way that words or preaching could never do.

CHAPTER 20

Building

a community

When George and Karin Hardy arrived at the Mission in 1960, George says, "I began to take a good look at things. The hotel had burned and all that property was available to us. Staff members were living in crowded conditions. The Mission was in dire need of more space for expansion and for accommodating both staff and guests."

After due consideration the hotel property was purchased, and George and another staff member, Corky Falk, began to draw plans to construct a building on the foundation. It would accommodate a newly-planned Bible School, have a gymnasium at one end and private accommodations on the upper floor.

Meanwhile, a fisherman told Elvin McMann, the hospital administrator, that the Canadian Fish Company at Nootka was going to give up its land. The fisherman said to Elvin, "Why don't you try to get the buildings?" Elvin discussed this with Dr. McLean and then wrote the company for information of the possibility of purchasing and moving the houses to Esperanza. An offer of $500.00 was made, along with the request for one other dwelling. No sooner had the letter been delivered, when a plane flew

View of ladies dormatory sawed in three pieces. One-third already transported by raft to Esperanza .

in with two men from the company. They spread out a large map of the site for Elvin and George, asking them to identify the bunkhouse and the other house they wanted. As they pondered this difficult choice, one of the company men took a red pen and circled all the houses at the camp. "Would you be willing to take all these houses for $1,000.00?" he said. Stunned at the offer, George and Elvin accepted immediately.

Dr. McLean, however, was not so overjoyed when he heard the news. "You'll never get the manager's house off the cliff. The living room is on twenty-foot pilings hanging out over the cliff," he said.

Although George had a cowboy background, he also had developed building skills. He said, "I had no idea how to get those buildings from Nootka to Esperanza, but the Lord did lay the responsibility of it squarely on my shoulders. And," he added, "I always did like a challenge."

In the spring of 1962 Corky began to build on the foundation of the former hotel. It was not as splendid a building as the hotel had been but it was extremely useful and well planned for its intended use.

The dedication of the building was held at the Annual Conference in Easter, 1964. Someone wrote, "On the old foundation, where stood a beer parlour, now stands a big building dedicated to God's service."

In the meantime, George Hardy had begun the work of clearing the land for the new homes. The Fleetwood Logging Company, from Little Zeballos, provided a Caterpillar bulldozer and operator. A road through the back side of the property had to be pushed through. The hill needed leveling, and access from the beach needed to be cleared and stumps blasted with dynamite. Huge rocks and trees needed to be cleared away.

Part-way up the hill a tiny shack had been built for Dudley Bowden, who was the teacher for the Bible School. During the summer months, when the work of clearing was underway, Dudley planned to take his holiday. Dudley was somewhat eccentric in appearance as well as in deportment. He had huge hands and feet attached to long legs and arms and a body that seemed loosely fitted together, but he was a man of great compassion and gentle spirit and his eccentric ways amused everyone.

When the morning of his departure came, he took his suitcases to the dock early, awaiting the arrival of the *Uchuck III*. Dudley did not want his freshly-pressed pants to be wrinkled before boarding the boat, so, he left them neatly folded over the back of a chair until it was time for departure. With his overcoat over his shirt, tie and underwear, he felt sufficiently dressed until the boat arrived. Then, he would have to put on only his pants, and depart.

The men were blasting stumps that day. George Hardy relates, "We drilled a hole under a stump on a hill not too far from Dudley's dwelling. We put a little dynamite under the stump but, when it went off, it didn't even put a crack in the stump. So we put in another charge but,

Marine ways with carpentry and mechanical wings.

Busy docks, 1974

this time, a little further under the stump. It was only a small charge, but it took the stump entirely out; and guess what else? Poor Dudley! His house was entirely blown to pieces—his pants along with it. (Fortunately, he had another pair in his suitcase at the dock—though wrinkled.)

As the clearing of the land progressed, communications with experts on the house-moving project were in progress. Quoted prices were astronomical. Many who assessed the job reported the undertaking to be impossible. Nevertheless, the need for added staff accommodation pressed urgently. So, with much prayer accompanied with limited manpower and limited resources, the decision was made that the staff would undertake the enormous task of moving the buildings—all of them.

Fleetwood Logging made skids which could be used to bring the houses from their hillside perches to the water level. The skids were made by lashing together logs two or three feet in diameter. These were placed length-wise under a house. Cross-logs were tucked under them to hold the frame rigid. A hydraulic jack was used to get the logs under the house. Alf Birtles relates, "We had to use every muscle we had to get those logs under those houses." When the logs were in place, the remaining old foundation had to be removed.

Amazingly, the first house to slide down on the skids to the raft was the manager's house. Alf recalls, "There is no way to describe just how those houses slid so gently down those rock cliffs and onto the raft. Every single building was safely rafted the 20 miles to Esperanza without one mishap. The women's dorm was sawed into three sections. The manager's house, also, was sawed into two sections. It was an incredible feat of endurance and innovation."

After the houses were beached at Esperanza, they had to be moved up the slopes to the prepared locations. To do this, a large winch was constructed using a six-cylinder Chevrolet engine and a transmission mounted on an existing winch body. This was a feat of engineering, a big undertaking by a small community on a limited budget, and a step forward in the Mission's growth.

To this day the houses continue to be well kept, and the white wood frame buildings are now a vital part of Esperanza.

. . . from the beach,1976

CHAPTER 21

Staff

joys and

struggles

*I*n the hearts of all the staff was a deep desire to know God and to serve Him well. Mrs. McLean had stated that, "it was a miracle whenever a new staff member came to Esperanza." She also expressed that "it also took a miracle to keep them working together when they did come."

Karin Hardy observed, "there have been a lot of things accomplished in each individual life during their time at the mission. Those who have seen what God has done at Esperanza know that He can make a difference."

***

Jan and "Corky" Falk were not prepared for the change of direction that was about to come into their lives while they were at Esperanza. Corky was keen to join Dr. McLean in his early-morning prayer hour but he just could not get up in time.

One night, he prayed, asking the Lord to awaken him so that he could go. Next morning he awoke and looked at the clock. The time was 5:45. He had 15 minutes to get there — but, the flesh was weak. His body could not make the effort. He went back to sleep.

Later in the day, he felt guilty. He was sure that his prayer had been answered, that the Lord had awakened him, and that he had simply not responded. Again he prayed, making the same request. Next morning he was awakened again but, this time, not so gently. He heard a loud knocking on the outside door. He lay there a few moments and, again, the loud knocking continued. He jumped out of bed, pulled on his trousers and hurried to see who was there. He was puzzled, for no one was at the door. He smiled, "Well, I'm out of bed, I might as well get to the prayer meeting."

At the prayer meeting a letter was read stating a need for a maintenance man for a mission in Africa. Corky's heart accelerated as he listened. Afterward, Mrs. Betty Sim, who was sitting beside him, said, "Corky, I think you're the man for that job in Africa." Corky was trembling with excitement, sensing that she was right.

He broke the good news of the position to Jan and, soon after, they left for mission studies at Prairie Bible Institute. They have been missionaries in Africa for many years now, and are presently living in Natal, South Africa.

⁂

Life in any small community has its difficulties as well as its joys. Esperanza was no exception. There were times of great conflict among the staff and there were times of loving intimacy. There were times when young people fell in love and were married. One fall, a young gentleman from Alberta had come to join George Hardy's crew to help in the relocation of the houses from Nootka to Esperanza.

A young nurse at the hospital caught his eye. Whenever a boat from the Mission took supplies or extra workers to Nootka, the young gentleman, Alf Birtles, made a point of sending a note to the young lady, Cathy McPherson, supposedly giving a report on the progress of their work.

After the moving was done and the houses were at Esperanza ready for finishing, he continued to show his interest in Cathy. As a nurse on the afternoon shift, she chose to eat her supper around 7:00 o'clock after the patients had been fed and things were quiet for awhile. Many times Alf was aware of her break and joined her, saying he might like a piece of toast or a snack of some kind.

Later, the winter storms arrived and drove the staff indoors for days on end. On Cathy's evenings off, Alf invited her to join him in one of the relocated houses he was working on. The house was not ready for occupancy but a new brick fireplace had been completed. It kept the living room warm and the two enjoyed many hours talking around the crackling fire.

By spring, Alf knew he wanted to marry Cathy. For some reason they had not talked much about their deep feelings. However, on a warm April night, Alf proposed. Cathy thought it was a joke and made light of his suggestion. Apparently, he became very serious and was deeply hurt by her response but he persisted and said to her, "Cathy, I really mean it! I love you and I want to marry you." She responded, "You mean this isn't an April Fool's joke?" He looked dismayed and said, "Oh, no! Is this April Fool's Day?" Together they laughed and embraced, relieving their joyful and loving feelings for each other that they had been keeping under control all winter.

Their wedding day came in August. Guests came by boat and by sea plane, from the island and from the mainland. The rose gardens were beautiful, with profuse blooms on the trailing red tea rose bushes. The yellow Peace roses were in full bloom. A warm, gentle breeze rustled in the maple leaves, the green grass and the variegated dahlia gardens were neatly manicured. It was a fairy-tale setting.

At the small, portable organ the organist played "The Wedding March." Guests in their summer finery sat on the big comfortable lawn chairs by the nurses' residence. Eventually, the porch door of the residence opened and the beautiful bride appeared on the arm of her father. Many guests dabbed their eyes, catching emotional tears as they escaped down their cheeks. All the guests rose to their feet.

A hush descended over the gathering as the bride and groom and their attendants, glowing in their youthful excitement, nervously took their places before the pastor, Rev. Bob Lilly. In a strong resonant voice, he began, "Dearly beloved, we are gathered here today . . ."

Suddenly he stopped.

Eyes of the guests widened as a bumble bee somehow flew between the layers of Cathy's dress. Swiftly, the bride's mother sprang into action. Kneeling down, she lifted Cathy's dress and began to shake the layers, one-by-one. The sound of buzzing was loud and persistent in this unexpected guest's frenzy to escape. Mouths agape, all watched in hushed suspense. Finally, freed at last, the insect buzzed the crowd and fled. When the applause and laughter died down, the ceremony continued — considerably more relaxed.

⚜

Sometimes, difficult relationships arose, not only from the isolation and overwork of the staff, but also from strained and unresolved personal relationships.

One lady told of her struggles in a strained relationship. "One day a speaker came to encourage us. During his message he stated, 'We suffer in our spirits when we don't forgive'. I sat there unable to listen to any more of the message"

The tension between her and one of her co-workers had become intolerable. She could not hide from the speaker's words and she could wait no longer. With a prayer for strength she stood up and, apologizing to the speaker, announced that she had something to say. Everyone looked at her in surprise.

The speaker graciously accommodated her interruption.
"I turned around and spoke directly to the one who had
caused me so much frustration. I told her that I was cross with
her and resented her. I told her I had suffered a lot with these
feelings towards her and probably she had, too, felt the same
towards me. But today I wanted to ask her forgiveness.
"From that day on, instead of avoiding each other, we were
able to be sympathetic and accepting of one another."

≈⊙≈

There were not only interpersonal tensions but also life-style
tensions. The 1960's brought change — radical change — to all
parts of Western culture, as the "Flower Children" made their
voices heard. Esperanza, though isolated, was not exempt.
The older ladies had established a strict dress code. Dresses
were worn at all times, even at Camp Ferrier. Slacks could be
worn only when gardening. Hair styles were severe — generally
braided and made into a bun at the back or on top of the head.
Makeup, especially lipstick, was frowned upon.
Some of the younger missionaries, coming from modern cities,
had never heard of such customs. Most did not own a house-
dress and were accustomed to wearing jeans. The dresses they
owned were very short (which was the style in the late 1960's
and early 1970's). This whole issue presented tension and conflict between the two groups of women, which in turn, divided
families. Background and life-style habits are not easily changed.
One night, at a party, this problem came to a head for the
ladies. As the games proceeded no one seemed very relaxed.
Spirits were gloomy, since every one attended by obligation
rather than by choice. Then, someone came up with an "ice-
breaker". A contest was introduced to determine who, among the
group, was wearing the shortest skirt. The idea seemed ridicu-
lous, since the younger women knew that only they were in the

contest; but the older more conservative women thought it would be interesting entertainment.

The group dissolved in laughter when it was Dr. McLean's daughter (we'll leave you to guess which one!) who won the prize. After this, an ease developed among the women. Differences in life style began to be accepted, resulting in a freer atmosphere. Wearing jeans or slacks gradually became acceptable attire after that.

Even Lillian Parry bought herself a pair of slacks and was not averse to asking many of the mission members, "How do I look?"

CHAPTER 22

Esperanza,
a continuing
hope

*T*hat September night in 1937, on the government dock in Victoria, as the *Princess Maquinna* cast off for her trip up the west coast, Mrs. McLean and her children had set out on a trusting journey into the unknown. The refrain of the hymn sung by the first friends of the Mission as they stood singing in the chilly night air floated to the ears of the departing McLean family. Those very words continue to underlie that early commission, "Take the name of Jesus with you."

As time passed, relationships and interactions among the staff of the Mission were often strained and tense. Weariness and loneliness crept into the lives of many at times. Understandably, sadness intensified as some were unable to cope with the crowded living conditions and the resulting inconveniences. Facing shortcomings in oneself, and accepting the struggles of others was difficult.

Dr. McLean and Earl Johnson knew deep sorrow in their hearts, feeling their own inadequacy in encouraging a continuous flow of congenial relationships and satisfactory living conditions for staff.

Esperanza is a name given to the area by the Spanish. Its meaning is "hope". Through the years in the midst of living our own lives and becoming involved in the lives of numerous others, hope has been available through prayer. A hope for today — A hope for tomorrow — A hope for the lost, the discouraged, the despairing, the ill. Sometimes, it radiated brighter than at other times. Without question, all who have participated in the endeavors of Esperanza bear witness to the personal sustaining power of the hope in Jesus Christ. All have been soothed and encouraged by the words Jesus spoke to His disciples: (John 14:1) "Do not let your hearts be troubled. Trust in God, trust also in me."

In this small corner of Vancouver Island, Esperanza's work is not yet complete. Years ago, Dr. McLean prayed to be sent to the toughest place on the West Coast. Perhaps you now understand why his wife took him by the lapel of his coat and asked, "Why on earth did you pray such a prayer?"

This book tells of the Esperanza we knew then and carry in our hearts now. It is comforting to know that the Esperanza of today, under the stewardship of the Shantymen's Christian Association is unchanged in its principles and in its commitment to the surrounding communities.

As Percy Wills and Dr. McLean first cried out to God in prayer for a hospital, prayer has continued to bring hope to not only those in prayer but to those being prayed for.

With a backward glance, let's await tomorrow by saying, Esperanza. There is hope!

Best friends — Jessie Smith and Elaine Stoik

AFTERWORD

I,
Louise Johnson,
do take thee...

*E*arl picked up the mail on the morning of that beautiful September day in 1971. After reading it quickly, he phoned me at work and asked if we could have lunch together. I knew he must have something important to discuss.

As we sat together sipping hot coffee in the cafeteria of the Seattle hospital, he removed an envelope from his pocket. Looking at me searchingly, he caused my curiosity to heighten.

"This will be a surprise to you," he said, removing the letter from the envelope.

As he read I could hardly believe what I was hearing. Dr. Herman A. McLean, founder of the Esperanza General Hospital, was inviting Earl to come to Esperanza and assume responsibility as superintendent of the Nootka Mission Association.

Earl was well acquainted with the Mission. For sixteen years, as a missionary with the Shantymen's Christian Association aboard the 50-foot mission vessel, *Messenger III*, he had visited the communities of the West Coast of Vancouver Island. Esperanza was the site of a busy hospital. Nootka Mission and the Shantymen were closely knit in purpose.

We sat together, considering Dr. McLean's letter. Many memories flashed through my mind . . .

Percy Wills, Harold Peters, Dr. McLean and their wives had become very dear to us. Percy and his wife Margaret had introduced Earl and me to each other while I was in nurse's training in Victoria, and we were married in 1955 following my graduation. Percy and Margaret had showered us with love and kindness in countless ways during our early years of adjustment to marriage and to ministry.

Harold Peters was like a father to Earl. They had lived, prayed, planned and sung together, hiking miles to visit isolated communities. Harold had trained Earl in the skills necessary for maneuvering the *Messenger* through the treacherous West Coast waters. Thinking of Harold brought such warm recollections to my mind: his sense of humour, his unique nautical vocabulary, his love for and familiarity with boats and the sea. I could see him in his red plaid, flannel shirt, under which he wore a white shirt, buttoned and exhibiting a neatly knotted tie.

Dr. McLean had celebrated his 60th birthday the year I met him. I had lived in a basement room in the McLean home, awaiting the birth of our oldest daughter, while Earl was organizing youth camps. The lifestyle in the McLean home included diligent prayer, hearty singing and gracious hospitality.

Interrupting my thoughts, Earl brought me back to the letter. "You are quiet, dear. What are you thinking?"

With the warm thoughts of these beloved people, I answered, "It's so pleasant just to be thinking of working on the West Coast again."

"Can I take that as a 'Yes'?", he said.

"Well, it's a definite 'maybe'," I responded, feeling a slight flow of excitement.

～～●～～

Earl had been pastoring on an interim basis in two Presbyterian churches while studying at Seattle Pacific University. Soon, he would be concluding his studies and, after graduation, would be looking for new challenges. He had experience as a sea-faring missionary and, as well, held a Master Seaman's ticket.

There were many things to consider and pray about in the next few weeks. Earl would be 41 years old that month and, since graduating from Prairie Bible Institute at the age of 22, he felt certain that he was to communicate the Gospel of the Lord Jesus Christ to the people in the isolated communities of Vancouver Island. With three children, Nancy, Deane and Diane, now in high school, their education would have to be carefully considered.

As soon as arrangements could be made, Earl and I visited Esperanza. A permanent commitment to a hospital and a community of about 50 people was a soul-searching quest.

It seemed a long ride, bouncing through the moderate swells whipped by the prevailing winds, cruising through Muchalet Inlet, passing Bligh Island and turning to our starboard into the Tahsis Inlet. Earl was delighted to point out the logging camps, Nootka Lighthouse and various islands, as we passed them. He also identified the rocks and reefs that he had carefully studied in years past.

The sky of Nootka Sound always seemed to be a deep beryl marine blue, a fascinating shade that was not only beautiful but also seemed to meet the sea and encompass the world and our surroundings with its power.

The water sparkled as the final energies of the sun beamed a few last rays to crown the waves it touched. The late afternoon sun stretched out the shadows of the giant evergreens, distorting their images in the wake of the boat's wash. Rounding the last bend in the journey, we watched the tiny white houses of Esperanza break into view — miniatures, against a gigantic backdrop of primeval forest with ancient granite towering far above.

Our decision was made. We committed our lives to Esperanza and all it stood for—to the people of the West Coast, to our own future, and most of all, to our Lord. That commitment was like a marriage vow:

> *for better, for worse*
> *for richer, for poorer*
> *in sickness and in health*
> *'til death do us part.*

✦❦✦

(Louise Johnson passed away on June 17, 1990).

Rose Ann Billy, Louise Johnson, Cecilia John, Dorothy John, Helen Carey, 1987

Index

N

Nanaimo sanitarium 66
Natal, South Africa 156
Nicolaye, Art 100
Nikolai, Dr. Egon 141
Nootka 149
Nootka Island 1, 13, 22
Nootka Lighthouse 165
Nootka Mission Association 60, 90,
      91, 94, 96, 139, 140
Nootka Mission Review 69
Nootka Sound 1, 2, 3, 9, 11, 91,
      104, 165
Nuchatlaht band 135
Nuchatlahts 1, 71, 99, 114, 120
Nuchatlahts Indian Reservation 114
Nuu-chah-nulth 1, 2, 10, 101

O

Otter Point 2, 3
Oxo box 10, 13

P

Parry, Lillian 133, 160
Patsy 136
Patton, Dr. Bob T. 140
Patton, Dr. Robert E. 134, 141, 143
Pauls, Dr. Vic 141, 146
Pauls, Joan 146
Penicillin 78
Penner, Dr. Ed 141
Penner, Lorna 129
Peters, Harold 40, 109, 164
Plummer, Howard 114
Port Alberni 4, 99, 113
Port Alice 50
Port Hardy 113
Port Renfrew 4
Portway, Ruth 75
potlatches 101

Prairie Bible Institute 4, 7, 69, 112,
      113, 156, 165
Prairie High School 50
Princess Maquinna 21, 27, 29, 36,
      50, 95, 104, 161
Privateer Mine 47

Q

Quadra,
      Juan Francisco de la Bodega y
      2
Queen's Cove 71, 99

R

raven 2
Rawstron, Dr. Grant 141
Ready, Mike and Rhea 139
Red Cross 9
Red Deer, Alberta 45
Reiger, Mr. George 140
Rhodes, Mrs. 69
Richardson, Hilda 75, 94, 106
Ritersgaard, Andy and Hilda 96
Rugged Point 54
Rustand, Mrs. 105

S

Saskatoon Bible College 76
School District No. 84 135
Scott, Dave and Marlene 133, 139
Sea Splendour 137
"Seaside" 127
Seattle Pacific University 165
Shane, Father 71
Shannon, Harold 35, 37, 49
Shantymen's Christian Association
      3, 4, 8, 30, 60, 89, 90, 91, 95,
      139, 162, 163
Sidney 45
Sim, Mrs. Betty 156
singing 123

Bibliography

This book has been made possible by the real-life participants of the story.

1. McLean, Marion (Doctor's wife) — made available her personal letters and files.
2. Rashleigh, Betty — made available her personal diary of Esperanza experiences.
3. Wills, Rev. Percy (Founder missionary) — made available many letters and clippings from papers.

Tape recorded interviews

1. Birtles, Alfred and Cathy — Calgary, Alberta. 1979
2. Falk, Corky — Natal, South Africa. 1980
3. Glaze, Ruth (McLean) — Victoria, B.C. 1980
4. Harmsworth, Neil and Kathy — Esperanza, B.C. 1984
5. McLean, Donnell — Japan. 1979
6. McPherson, Dan — Whitby, Ontario. 1985
7. Sutherland, Bob and Shirley (McLean) — Terrace, B.C. 1984
8. Adams, James — Ahousat, B.C. 1978
9. Boughton, Dr. Keith and Nancy — Kamloops, B.C. 1981
10. Carlile, Fanny (R.N.) — Victoria, B.C. 1979
11. Hardy, George and Karin — Victoria, B.C. 1980
12. Hill, Jack and Myrna — MV Anastasis, Mercy Ship YWAM 1981
13. Johnson, Earl — Esperanza, B.C. 1979

14. McLean, Mrs. Marion — (Deceased 1987) 1979
15. McMann, David — Gold River, B.C. 1985
16. Morrison, Lou (R.N.) — Victoria, B.C. 1979
17. Parry, Lillian — (Deceased). 1979
18. Pauls, Dr. Vic — Vancouver, B.C. 1980
19. Peters, Harold — Union Bay, B.C. 1980
20. Wills, Rev. Percy — (Deceased 1991) 1979 (Two tapes)
21. Collection of experiences as related by various staff. 1979
22. Collection of experiences as related by various staff — Homecoming, two tapes, 1981